Textual Activism

Rabbi Mike Moskowitz

Copyright © 2019 Congregation Beit Simchat Torah
130 West 30th Street, New York, NY 10001
www.cbst.org

All rights reserved.

Cover Photo: Harold Levine

ISBN: 9781798034507

To my children and for all of God's children.

CONTENTS

Acknowledgments	vii
Foreword	ix
Introduction	1

Passover

Answering the Transgender Son	4
Not Everything is as It Appears	7
Redeeming Religion from Slavery	10
A Passover Message from the Southern Border	12
All Who Were Silenced, Let Them Come Speak	17

Lag B'Omer

Hillula to Her Heart	22

Shavuot

Transgender and Transcendent	26
Cisgender Humility and Accepting the Torah	29
Rabbinic Responsibility for LGBTQ Jews	32
Speaking About AIDS on Shavuot	35

Three Weeks

Rosh Chodesh and Rabbisplaining	37
9th of Av Letter to Day Schools	39
Moral Mincha - Protesting Outside of the Orthodox Union	41

Rosh Hashanah

Rosh Hashanah: A Time for Divine Consent	45
Coming of Age as Gender Non-Conforming	49
New Years Resolution	53

Expanding the "We" for Rosh Hashanah	55
Educating the Yated	58

Sukkot
Sukkot, Security, and Trans Rights	60
The Cloud of Glory	63

Chanukah
What Do You Want Your Candle To Be?	65
Building a Temple From Tears	67
Coming Together Against Hate	70

Shevat
Rosh Chodesh Shevat and DACA	73
Renewal and Rebirth	76

Purim
Back to the Garden: Purim, Patriarchy, and a Path Forward	79
I Am a Boy and These Are My Clothes	82

Allyship
Noah's Ark: A Failed Ally-ship	86
Allyship as Spiritual Practice	88
Advancing The Rabbinic Prescription For Transgender Health Care	91
Shabbos Shows Us How to "Chaver Up"	95
What the Torah and Talmud Teach Us About Calling Transgender People By Their Names	98
Queer Advice from Straight Rabbis	101
I'm an Orthodox Rabbi Marching with Pride	105
Wanting to Get it Right for Pride	107
One Straight, White, Cisgender Rabbi's Role as an Ally	110
Transitioning Towards God	113
Wrestling with Mourning on Transgender Day of Remembrance	119

World AIDS Day and the Role of the Righteous	122
In Dark Times, Be a Light	125
How Goodly are Your Rainbow Tents	128
The Torah of Action	131
It's a Big Torah	133

Rabbinic Failures

Corruption and Greed Get in the Way of the Torah	136
Orthodox Jews and the Child Victims Act	139
Healing the Afflictions of Separation	141

Interfaith

Interfaith Leaders Stand Up for Yes on 3 Campaign	145
The Audacious and Inspirational Gift of Pride	148
Opening Doors and Hearts on Transgender Day of Visibility	151
Faith Leaders Must Stop Acting As If There's No Preventing Natural Disasters	155
Faith in the Face of Fear	158

Speeches and Interviews

Homophobia in Orthodoxy	161
Responding to Trans Erasure	164
Religiously Non-Conforming – Unorthodox Podcast	166
The Rabbinic Voice of Allyship – Here & Now	172

Aggadah

Above and Below the Binary	176
Balancing Solo and Communal Jewish Practice	205

Credits 230

ACKNOWLEDGMENTS

Like God, we are known and identify ourselves in many different ways. Also like God, we are singular and one of a kind. I would like to acknowledge and give thanks to the Source of all life, experiences, and expressions. Mine, like yours, is unique.

This small offering intends to share some of the insights that have inspired me as a rabbinic voice for allyship in spiritual practice.

I have been blessed to be guided by the wisdom of tradition and the many teachers of that wisdom along the way. May this bring joy to them and glory to the One we all journey to know.

My wonderful friends at Kehilat Harlem hosted me for a weekly class we called "Textual Activism" which looked to rabbinic and mystical texts as energizing fuel for advancing our work in social justice. The title was suggested to me by my dear friend Taya Shere, co-founder of Kohenet Hebrew Priestess Institute. Many of the thoughts contained in these essays were developed in preparation for those classes. Rabbi Menachem Creditor was very kind in assisting with the technical aspects of publishing and an encouraging voice along the way.

I identify as many things, however a writer is not one of them. Rabbi Rachel Barenblat and Seth Marnin were both exceedingly generous with their time and support in editing many of these articles before they were published. I am also so grateful for your friendship and guidance.

Shari Motro has challenged me, and countless others, to expand and develop our voice through writing. It hasn't always been easy, but it's always a pleasure.

Steven Philp added a level of professionalism and

consistency to this book as an editor and designer. It has been such a gift to work with you on this project. We are all so excited for your rabbinate to begin and your incredible talents to continue improving the world!

The entire CBST staff, and especially Izzy Levy for their help with the manuscript and Tasha Calhoun for constant daily support, has made this past year possible and a pleasure. I am so honored to be a member of this incredible team.

Over the last several years I have lost many friends, rabbis, and communities. I am grateful, beyond words, to those who have remained from my years in Yeshiva and in my hometown of Richmond, VA. Your support has made all the differnce.

When you are on the right path, you often meet the right people. It has been an amazing experience to be in partnership with the wonderful folks at Bayit. Rabbis David, Evan, Rachel, and gang - thank you for the opportunity to be part of your holy work of building accessibility in Jewish life.

Last January, when I was arrested with a group of rabbis in support for DACA, I met one of the great leaders of our people, Rabbi Sharon Kleinbaum, in the back of a police wagon. She, with the generous support of CBST and its members, created a new position to host my advocacy as the Scholar-in-Residence for Trans and Queer Jewish Studies. I am eternally grateful for your friendship, mentorship, and courage. In the words of Rabbi Akiva: "Mine and yours are hers."

To my mother, who has always believed in me and has been a constant and unwavering buoy my entire life, thank you. The Hebrew word for faith, *emunah*, has its root in the word *em*, mother, and so too, the roots of my faith also come from my mother. May you have *Yiddishe Nachas* from all of us.

FOREWORD
By Rabbi Sharon Kleinbaum

In January of 2018, I was in Washington, D.C. with a small group from Congregation Beit Simchat Torah to participate in the holy work of protesting the United States' treatment of DACA recipients, and of immigrants in general. We came to protest because we understood it as an obligation, both because of what God demands of us and because of what our history as a people has taught us. Care for the stranger. Never again means never again for everyone.

We were also there representing our community back in New York City - an LGBTQ synagogue welcoming of all sexual orientations and gender identities. After gathering with a group of Jews from all over the country, over 80 of us (including three from CBST), were arrested in the Russell Senate Office building. We were arrested as Jews, some of us as LGBTQ Jews. We were arrested singing and praying.

After being arrested, ten of us were placed handcuffed in one police van. I knew that this could be a very long process, so I asked if someone in the van had some Torah to teach. Most of us in that van were rabbis. The black hatted, bearded rabbi sitting across from me volunteered to teach.

Now I must say, I have been deeply engaged in the work of the liberation of LGBTQ Jews for over 30 years. I've taught Torah through an LGBTQ lens, I've studied and taught "fairy tales," and I've studied and taught queer Torah. When the Haredi rabbi said he wanted to teach something about trans lives and textual understanding of gender, I was a little skeptical.

But what I heard then proverbially knocked me off

the metal bench of that police van. Here was a shiur that was new, fresh, deep, profound, and exciting. The rabbi was using text in an entirely new way – gutsy and bold. He was reading these texts in a way that made clear that God loved trans people.

That rabbi turned out to be Mike Moskowitz.

In the many hours that it took the police to process us, I got to know Mike Moskowitz's story. I learned that, as a result of his teaching and advocacy on behalf of trans people, he had been fired from his positions as a rabbi of a synagogue and college campus and was now working in a deli. I learned his painful story of transformation from clueless cisgender, straight rabbi to deep ally. I learned his deeply human personal story of the pain of relationships, parenting, and struggling with his community.

I came back to CBST committed to finding a way to bring Rabbi Moskowitz to our community. Luckily for us, a wonderful CBST couple stepped up to help us bring Rabbi Moskowitz to the synagogue, and the rest is history. In the less than one year that Rabbi Moskowitz has served as CBST's Scholar-in-Residence for Trans and Queer Jewish Studies, he has transformed the Jewish landscape for trans and non-binary Jews everywhere. He is both deeply traditional and radically progressive, a vocal advocate for trans inclusivity and an ally to the LGBTQ community. As an Ultra Orthodox rabbi at an LGBTQ synagogue, he brings a unique perspective and frame of reference, and we have been so fortunate to have a scholar of his caliber here at CBST. He has written and published many articles, helping to create an intellectual framework to change and deepen the discussion, especially within – but not limited to – the Orthodox world.

With this book, we are proud to gather together so many of these works of intellectual, spiritual, and activist Jewish depth that will bring glory to God and change the world.

TEXTUAL ACTIVISM

הָפַכְתָּ מִסְפְּדִי לְמָחוֹל לִי פִּתַּחְתָּ שַׂקִּי וַתְּאַזְּרֵנִי שִׂמְחָה:
לְמַעַן ׀ יְזַמֶּרְךָ כָבוֹד וְלֹא יִדֹּם יְהוָה אֱלֹהַי לְעוֹלָם אוֹדֶךָּ:

You have transformed my lament into dancing for me, You undid my sackcloth and girded me with gladness. So that my soul might sing to You and not be stilled, Hashem, my God, forever will I thank You. (Psalms 30:12-13)

Rabbi Sharon Kleinbaum,
Senior Rabbi Congregation Beit Simchat Torah

INTRODUCTION

My journey to allyship, like most, is deeply personal and still ongoing. Several years ago someone in my family announced that they were transitioning from one gender to another. I so desperately wanted to be supportive and yet had no idea how. It was immediately clear to me that the stakes were high and that I was not at all equipped to be adequately helpful.

I had never struggled with or even thought of my own gender identity. Now, having obsessively sat with it ever since, I have evolved to a place of knowing that my lack of awareness of gender in lived experience beyond my physical body is part of what makes me cisgender and not transgender. Realizing these limitations has sharpened my commitment to humble listening.

That year I listened a lot. I listened to anyone who would share their story and wisdom. I also heard the deafening silence from my rabbinic community when I reached out for guidance. A turning point for me was when I was speaking to one of the truly great educators of our generation (an amazing human whom I've been a student of for 20 years) and he told me: "I just don't know. I've never been asked this before." If he didn't have the answers, who would?

There is obvious tension at the intersection of tradition and innovation. If we change the rules too much, it's a different game. But if we don't adapt, no one will show up to play. As an Orthodox Jew, I believe that the Torah was revealed to Moses on Mt. Sinai by God and is eternal, infinite, and immutable. For me, this also means that God had conversations with Moses about trans experiences in Jewish thought and law and we are here to uncover and discover that Divine Will.

In Yeshiva I was taught that religion is the process of being in a relationship with God. Judaism is the relationship God intends to have with the Jewish people and the Torah contains the details of that relationship.

When done properly, religion can be the container to help support a healthy and happy partnership with God. It can be comforting, soothing, and deeply nourishing. Unfortunately, too often religion is used to separate us from God and "religious" communities. We are overdue for a restorative religion that empowers each individual to own and embrace a relationship with a God who waits and yearns for us to be present as our whole selves, the result of all of our identities and life experiences.

Judaism is monotheistic, but not monolithic. God has many names and attributes, often gendered, and also God just *is*. My God is an all gender God as opposed to a gender neutral God. Many of the essays in this book invite us to question if gender exists on a soul level as part of God.

Judaism is a gender based spiritual practice, and recognizes that men and women are not exactly the same or there wouldn't be space to transition. Where their true differences end and the social construction of gender begins is not always clear and there are many questions that still need to be answered. However, there is no doubt to the urgent need and moral obligation for religious communities to support and protect those who are being dehumanized.

For me, the mystical tradition offers a portal into a more idealistic reality constructed from a purer spiritual periodic table of elements. The better we can understand how the world came to be broken, the easier it is for us to come together to fix it. Part of the work of rebuilding is recognizing that our intentions assist in defining the impact of our efforts.

Insights help provide our outlook. Many of the

articles in this book contain allusions to truths that are concealed and housed through the Hebrew Alphabet. Gematria, a system of calculating the numerical value of Hebrew letters, is often understood as a way to excavate deeper meaning. Tradition teaches that these are not invented but rather are a reflection of pre-existing objective truths.

An ideal Jewish education is one that provides, at a minimum, a level of self sufficiency and proficiency that parallels one's secular and academic achievements. The more that we are able to know about God's desires and the wisdom contained within, the more we are able to make informed decisions that can bring us and this world closer to God.

Allyship is awkward. Stepping forward from a place of privilege to help others is predicated on the world being broken and people mistreating each other. We all have the ability to ally - חבר up to ease the suffering and oppression of others and work towards a more just, equitable, and sustainable humanity. As we continue to heal from the trauma of religion, I've found it helpful to cope by trying to effect change. Grounding this holy revolution through our texts helps us continue expanding our tradition and amplifying God's voice in this world. Let's listen to the charge of Hillel, זיל וגמור… get textually active!

PASSOVER

ANSWERING THE TRANSGENDER SON[1]

Last year, an hour before Passover began, a 7 year-old boy of trans experience, who was given a female name at birth, asked: "Tatty, can you please call me 'Dew?'" "Of course," the father said, but that response felt inadequate. The Haggadah offers how we might respond to the child who is wise, wicked, simple, or silent but it doesn't provide an answer for the daughter who asks to be a son.

When the Talmud can't resolve a question it concludes the conversation with a declaration: תיק״ו. This word is an acronym for תישבי יתרץ קושיות ויאבעיות, or "The Tishbite will answer questions and inquiries." This individual from the ancient town of Tishbi is none other than the prophet Elijah, who is called Eliyahu HaNavi, Eliyahu HaTishbi. There is a tradition that he is also the author of the Haggadah. How might the great prophet help the parent answer the child who asks, "Why am I different from all other children?"

In this world of pain, suffering, and darkness we often have many more questions than answers. God appears to be hidden and yet we have faith. On the night of Passover we are transported to a future time when God is revealed and all is made clear; the night actually becomes like day. Elijah, we are told, will be sent to usher in this messianic era. We open the door for him during the Seder because in that moment we have already arrived in a futuristic time. It is no coincidence that the song *"Chad*

---

[1] Originally published on April 5, 2017 by the Jewish Orthodox Feminist Alliance Blog, under the pen name Kol Raychaim

Gadya" at the end of the Haggadah is written in past tense – "Then the Blessed One came and killed the Angel of Death" – because on the Seder night we temporarily exist in a time when God has brought the promise of eternal life to fruition.

On the night of Passover there is no longer tension. The unity of God's many characteristics is exposed and embraced. The song "אחד מי יודע?" – "Who Knows One?" – teaches that divinity is singular. God is one, perfect, and without division. The numerical value of אחד (echad) is 13, the same as the Hebrew word for love, אהבה (ahavah). In the Haggadah, we find the word אחד (echad) introduces each of the four children: אחד חכם ואחד רשע ואחד תם ואחד אינו יודע לשאול – one who is wise, one who is wicked, one who is simple, and one who does not know how to ask.

To explain this repetition our tradition teaches that the uniting power of love, אהבה (ahavah), shows us that there aren't four children, but rather one child, who - like all people - contains multiple contradicting parts: wise, wicked, simple, and silent. 4 x 13 is 52, the numerical value of the word בן (ben), or child. It is not coincidental that the name Elijah, אליהו, also equals 52 for he is the harbinger of peace, שלום (shalom), which can also be translated as wholeness. In the messianic era, our disparate parts - like the different aspects of God - will be become unified.

"Dew" is the third child in his family. 3 x 13 – the value of love, אהבה (ahavah) – is 39. This is also the numerical value of טל (tal), which means dew. On the first day of Passover we say the prayer for טל (tal). The Talmud tells us that the keys for releasing dew were given to Elijah. טל (tal) is emblematic of God's loving kindness. Dew never ruins crops or inhibits travel, but rather refreshes the earth and allows for things to grow. It emanates only goodness. The verse blesses us that the heavens shall drip with dew. Isaac blessed Jacob, his son, with this on the first night of

Passover. Tal is a blessing.

I don't know how the parent should answer the child who asks, "Why am I different from all other children?" But Elijah the Prophet provides us with some guidance for this תיק״ו, unresolved question: to respond with compassion. So when the child asks "Tatty, can you see me the way that I do?" perhaps we should answer them: "I see you the way that God does: with complete love."

NOT EVERYTHING IS AS IT APPEARS[2]

The holiday of Passover invites us to enhance our vision, especially in the darkness. Like searching for chametz (leaven) by candlelight, we are asked to peer into the nooks and crannies of our lives; to see beyond the superficial, rejecting the names, appearances, and labels that curb complexity and identity. We often encounter the limits of language, but on Passover (in Hebrew "*peh sach*" — "a mouth that speaks") words are meant to expand and reveal what is normally hidden.

International Transgender Day of Visibility (TDOV) is an annual holiday that falls every year on March 31st, and this year, 2018, it coincides with the first day of Passover. TDOV is a time to celebrate the lives of transgender and gender non-conforming people around the globe and their courage to live authentically, while also raising awareness of the discrimination and violence these individuals continue to face.

The Passover Seder offers us a chance to explore and hold together contradictions, to raise up and make visible what is often obscured, and to honor the complexity of our lives. It is a holiday of asking questions and seeking answers. We only need to look as far as the Seder table. From the four cups of wine to the bitter herbs, every aspect of the Seder holds multiple allusions, explanations,

---

[2] Originally published on March 13, 2018 as "Not Eveything is As It Appears to Be: A Guided Discussion for Passover & International Transgender Day of Visiblity" by the Times of Israel Blog, co-authored with Seth M. Marnin

and secrets - realities that are often hidden, sometimes too vulnerable to be exposed. We cover and uncover the matzah. We hold it up, break open the middle one, and look deep inside. On the superficial level, matzah is just unleavened bread. On Passover, it is both the bread of affliction and the bread of redemption - simultaneously and without any contradiction. So too, the charoset, which is a sweet mixture of honey, nuts, and apples but also represents the mortar Jews used to join bricks together when we were enslaved in Egypt.

Transgender people often experience visibility in complicated and even contradictory ways. Being seen as one's authentic self brings great joy and contentment; to be respected for who you are is a particularly powerful experience for a transgender person. But sometimes being seen is extremely dangerous. In 2017 advocates found that the deaths of at least 28 transgender individuals in the United States were due to violence; in 2018, we already know of six transgender people who have have been killed. Like the matzah or charoset, these two realities exist simultaneously.

Here are some questions you might want to consider discussing at your Seder:

For each question, think about the multiplicity of your own identities. How might you answer these questions in different environments (home, work, religious community, etc.)? How and why might people who are different from you—whether because of their race, age, gender, gender identity, religion, religious identity, sexual orientation, immigration status, disability, to name a few — think differently about these questions?

What does it mean to be seen?
What do we show people about ourselves?
What parts of ourselves do we keep hidden?
How does it feel when someone really sees you?
What are some of the perceived contradictions in our own identifies?

The Hebrew word "to see," *yireh*, is related to the word for "awe," *yirah*. The more we see beyond the superficial to understand the reality of life and creation, the more reverence we have for its Creator and the more responsibility we feel to protect it. On Passover we should endeavor to respond to darkness as God did in the beginning: by creating light. Our collective need to be seen and understood isn't a human virtue that separates us from God or each other. Rather, it echoes God's desire to fill the primordial emptiness and void by creating us—*b'tzelem elohim*—in God's image, so that God should be better seen and understood just as we all wish to be.

On Transgender Day of Visibility and on Passover, we focus on our stories, our voices, our beings. At the Seder, all are welcome to be seen for the unique blend we bring to the world as a reflection of our divine source. We see you, our transgender siblings. We are in awe of you. For all those who feel invisible, come and be seen.

REDEEMING RELIGION FROM SLAVERY

"If she wants to wear a dress and sit in the women's section, she is welcome to come to shul," said the rabbi of my [old] synagogue, in Lakewood, NJ informing me of the newly revealed policy of trans-exclusion. Using the wrong pronoun to help reinforce his transphobic reality, the rabbi told me that congregants were complaining and he had assured them that he would take care of it – "it" being a trans child, wearing a yarmulke and tzitzit, praying quietly next to his father in shul.

I was prepared for my response, but not for his. As soon I began to defend the permissibility and obligation of trans-inclusivity, from within Jewish law, he quickly interrupted me by saying "This is not about Halacha; it is about people feeling uncomfortable."

"People," evidently, is a rabbinic term limited to include only those who have socially constructed rights and are afraid of losing them. This rabbi wants to create a safe space for the privileged, entitled, and empowered so they can continue with their exceptional experience of comfort at the expense of those who are the most marginalized, discriminated against, and oppressed.

Today is Rosh Chodesh Nissan, the month that celebrates the breakthrough of the miraculous into what we had assumed was the natural order, transforming subjugation and constraint into equality, both in Biblical times and today. "נס," *Neis* or miracle, is the Hebrew root of the month's name, alludes to revolting against the status

---

[3] Originally published on March 16, 2018 by *Tikkun*

quo of oppression, rising up, and elevating the downtrodden. These two letters invite us to be part of the miraculous revolution of restorative religion, just as God corrected the injustice of our slavery in Egypt.

In the alphabetic acrostic of Psalm 145, Ashrei, the letter "נ" is the only letter that is absent; because it represents נפילה, falling. It is for that reason that the next line starts with "ס" , "Supporting all those who have fallen." The "ס" , resembling a circle, is the ubiquitous symbol for equality, as every place on the circumference is equidistant from the epicenter. This is the banner (also נס in Hebrew) of our national struggle, to recognize that all people are created equal, and the charge of today's spiritual resistance.

The "ס" is also the 15th letter in the Hebrew alphabet, which corresponds to the 15 steps of the Haggadah that we read on the 15th day of this month. This is when the moon is at its fullest, reflecting the light of its source - which should inspire us to do the same. This year, the first day of Passover is also Trans Day of Visibility.

When conversations about access to sacred spaces have nothing to do with God then there is nothing sacred about the space nor the conversation. However, if we can recenter our priorities, seeing the physical needs of another as part of our spiritual service, then even in mundane spaces there is much holiness. Nissan is a call to refocus our sights on those who have been denied equality and free all those who are still enslaved by the many systems of oppression present in society. When one is accustomed to discrimination, equality feels like liberation.

A PASSOVER MESSSGE FROM THE SOUTHERN BORDER[4]

During the Seder there is a universal custom to recount the 10 plagues while spilling out a drop of wine for each one. The first plague is *dam*, blood. Why is this the first plague? We learn that all of the Egyptians were punished through the Nile turning into blood because Pharaoh decreed that the Hebrew children should be separated from their parents and drowned. The commentators ask, "Why was the entire nation punished if it was only a few people who actually carried out the decree?" Because responsibility falls on the community. As Rabbi Abraham Joshua Heschel writes: "In a free society, few are guilty, all are responsible."

From those days to this day, we understand as Jews and human beings that we as individuals are not exempt from owning the darkest sins of our community. Whether we participate, whether we are passive, or whether we protest — while we remain accountable, we have the power to determine our response.

It's been two weeks since we landed in El Paso, beginning our journey to the Southern border, including Texas, New Mexico, and Mexico, with the HIAS and T'ruah clergy delegation.

Just as Moses saw God and didn't have the proper words, so too do we find ourselves lacking in accurate and emotive descriptions for what we witnessed. While

---

[4] Originally published on April 19, 2019 by *Gay City News*, co-authored with Rabbi Yael Rapport.

acknowledging that words limit, our feelings were expansive and overwhelming in ways that our retelling can give no justice. Not only at this moment, but also in the moment of walking through the sterile and staged holding cells of Otero Detention Center and Southwest Key Children's Shelter, we felt hopelessness, impotency, despair — trapped in a performative role of observation and internalization, not action, not change-making.

Otero and Southwest Key are both opportunist, for-profit businesses, incentivized by the exploitation of others. MTC, Management and Training Corporation, a part of the prison industrial complex that operates a US prison on the same site for violent offenders, makes $97 dollars a day per head on each of the more than 1,000 individuals being held at Otero. "Inmates," as they are called at Otero, work for a dollar a day doing everything from barbering to packing sandbags outdoors in the New Mexico sun. A tapped phone call home, on prison phones, costs 33 cents a minute. Inmates can only speak to lawyers using translation services, which are in-house — meaning tapped. Medical care is available on site, but the one doctor who serves the entire population only works 24 hours a week. A complaint by the American Civil Liberties Union has already been filed against the treatment of LGBTQ individuals being held, who are frequently isolated in solitary confinement "for their own protection" and subject to abuse and harsher working conditions.

To be perfectly clear, seeking asylum in the United States as these "inmates" have done, is NOT and is never a crime.

Over the course of the Seder, the four cups of wine that we drink have their scriptural source in the four languages of redemption described in Exodus — the "*Arba L'Shonot shel Geula.*" God says, "I will redeem you, I will take you out, I will save you, and I will bring you to me." Part of the liberation of people is the emancipation of language. Passover expands our capacity to elevate the language we use to describe people and circumstances. In fact, the word Pesach — *"peh sach"* — means "the mouth that speaks." All of the mitzvot of the Seder, whether eating, storytelling, or asking questions, focus on developing this ability. The way in which we talk about things affects the way we see them, and Pesach is our opportunity to see with clarity.

As we moved through different worlds of experience at the Southern border, we heard four languages used to describe those who sought safety and sanctuary in this country. Each description offered a different perspective, not only on the circumstance of the individual but how language affects the way we see people and our response to their struggle.

In Otero, the warden, the ICE official who followed our group, the community representative from Chaparral, New Mexico, and the Detention Center chaplain referred to "inmates" and "detainees."

Reuben Garcia, the director for decades of Annunciation House, an El Paso shelter that houses and places more than 600 individuals and families every day who are released from ICE and Border Patrol custody, called those he serves "refugees" — a political, purposeful statement, as he believes the US holds a moral and legal responsibility under international agreement to afford refugee status to anyone from Central America who is seeking asylum.

At Las Americas, the El Paso Immigration Advocacy Center, lawyers, advocates, and activists called their clients "immigrants" and "asylum seekers."

We heard new language at the Hope Border Institute and Casa del Migrante — a shelter in Juarez, Mexico, which houses and protects the 10,000 people awaiting processing in the US, including those who had over years built lives, families, and futures here, who had still been deported. The name of the institution and the descriptor for those who reside there is "migrants." By describing a "person in movement," such a name can encompass those too who are victims of forced displacement within national boundaries, an all too common event in Central and South America, and calls attention to the larger question of human migration, an ancient reality encompassing violence, global geopolitics, and climate change. "Migrant" stems from the same root as the Spanish "migrantes," which is the way those at the shelter refer to themselves.

Language can unify and language can divide. The way we describe a person or a circumstance can draw us closer to identifying with them, or can shape them into the other — creating distance and distaste. The night of the Seder reminds us of our perpetual communal responsibility to use words to bring people together. That's what we are doing on Passover; not just going through the motions of a historical retelling, but reliving and relating as if in a first-person experiential narrative. We say *"B'chol dor vador,"* in every generation it is REQUIRED of us to see ourselves as if we were the ones going forth from Egypt.

How in this generation can words and deeds shift us closer to those telling the same story today — the story of crossing a desert, leaving all we know behind, in search of a promise that brings us out of narrow places? It is their story, it is our story, it is the human story.

What language will you choose to use to describe those affected by immigration and migration today?

Can you join us at Congregation Beit Simchat Torah as our community accompanies those with local ICE deportation hearings, trains ourselves in the legal mechanism of citizenship application, and advocates for policy change in the halls of power and through our calls and cards?

Could you send badly needed supplies to Southern border shelters, such as travel-size toiletries for those recently released, or adult and kids underwear in sizes small and medium?

Chayavim anu — we are bound, and we are not free

until all are free. This Passover, let us add a new chapter to our ancient tale that brings us to today, let us choose around our Seder tables the ways we use our gifts, our words, and our power to bring others into a *z'man cheiruteinu*, a time of liberation.

ALL WHO WERE SILENCED, LET THEM COME SPEAK[5]

At its best, the Passover Seder can model the values it celebrates—freedom from slavery and oppression—by disrupting habitual hierarchies and bolstering inclusivity. Unfortunately, sometimes our attempts to honor this sacred mission fall short. At its worst, the festive meal celebrating freedom can deepen the very divisions it seeks to heal.

For those who wish to create a meaningfully inclusive Seder, traditional sources offer a wealth of inspiration, and encourage each generation to add its own creative voice to the practice. Here are some suggestions as to how to make a traditional Seder more inclusive:

Remember that it's a communal effort

Seder means "order." It revolves around a script—the Haggadah—that offers a particularly promising spiritual technology to empower the disempowered. At many Seders, the reading of the Haggadah moves around the table so that every voice is heard.

Amplify marginalized voices

By common custom, the youngest child is the one who asks the four questions—ensuring that children are integrated into the ritual as soon as they are able to speak

---

[5] Originally published on March 23, 2018 as "How To Host A Truly Inclusive Passover Seder" by the *Forward,* co-authored with Shari Motro

and encouraging adults to listen to voices that are sometimes ignored. Through the story of the four children - wise, wicked, simple, and silent - the Haggadah reserves a place at the table for different members of our community, even the rebellious child who turns their back on tradition. Some hosts invite members of other faiths, refugees, and the indigent to join the meal. Many leave the door open and set an extra place at the table for the prophet Elijah—invoking the radical invitation: "All who are hungry, let them come and eat."

Encourage participation through listening circles

As every teacher knows, in group settings some people will not participate unless they are explicitly invited. The silent are often women, minorities, or simply introverts. Sometimes silence is a choice, and that should be respected. But all too often, group dynamics unintentionally replicate existing hierarchies, intensifying instead of healing the pain of those who feel like strangers.

It's time to reclaim the Seder as the creatively inclusive practice it has the potential to be.

The medieval philosopher Maimonides calls on every person to retell the story of the Exodus - the more the better. To disrupt default patterns, Maimonides' words may be interpreted as a call to supplement the Seder with listening circles.

A listening circle is a group dialogue that supports deep listening and speaking from the heart. It is not a debate nor is it an analytical conversation in which we are trying to solve a problem or reach agreement on an issue. The goal is to create a safe space for people of diverse backgrounds to share their unique gifts and perspectives.

The Native American version of this practice employs a "talking stick" to designate the speaker. At the Seder, any object that carries symbolic value can be used as a "talking piece"—like matzah (unleavened bread symbolizing humility), or an orange (symbolizing inclusion of women and members of the LGBT community).

Four questions can serve as a guide to four listening circles throughout the evening, with each question following one of the four cups of wine.

What is your name — the name you wish to be called tonight?

Names imbue us with dignity. They serve as the prelude to the book of Exodus (its Hebrew title, Shemot, also means names) to teach us that, before slavery, people had names. But the story of Moses begins with a glaring absence of names. We read about a woman who gives birth to a boy, a sister who watches as he floats alone in treacherous waters, a daughter of a tyrant who draws him out – all of them nameless. Only once he is adopted does Moses receive his name.

The first step of the Seder, Kadesh, means sanctification. One way to sanctify a community is to recognize its individual members by their preferred name. Some of us, like Moses (which means drawn from the water), were given a name. Others, like Abraham and Sarah, have changed our names after life-altering transitions. Some use multiple names, pronunciations, or pronouns. What is the name that supports your experience of freedom tonight?

What is your personal experience of Egypt?

The second cup of wine follows the Magid, the telling of the Exodus from Egypt, our passage out of the ultimate constriction. The second listening circle we propose invites people to share a story of oppression. Speaking about trauma can be difficult; people should feel free to answer the question indirectly. The prompts are suggestive, not rigid prescriptions, and sharing in a listening circle is always optional—you can always simply pass the talking piece along. If you do choose to share, try to speak in the first person. Limiting statements to "I statements," rather than speaking as representatives, honors others in the circle—they have agreed to listen, not to be spoken for.

What are you thankful for?

Barech—the grace after the meal — as well as the search for the afikoman (the activity that for many children represents the high point of the night), offer an opportunity for people to share a story of gratitude. The third question asks: What blessings are you thankful for tonight?

What does 'miracle consciousness' mean to you?

After Hallel, the readings that praise God, we invite people to take the final step out of slave consciousness by cultivating miracle consciousness: Have you ever witnessed a miracle? Stories of coincidences, survival against the odds, unexpected love, or dreams of ultimate redemption can all contribute to this final round of the evening.

At a large Seder there might be time for just one of the questions, or questions may be answered in pairs or in triads. And different questions might be more fitting depending on the people gathered.

Dialogue is difficult — and that's okay.

We recognize that the listening circle format might make some people uncomfortable—including in allowing for slower speech and even silence. Change is rarely easy, but the invitation to stretch out of our comfort zone is at the very heart of what Passover is all about.

After the Exodus, when the Israelites were wandering through the desert, some complained to Moses: it would have been better had you left us to die in Egypt. The change was so shocking to them, that they missed the familiarity of slavery.

Passover acknowledges the tension that comes with change, and it encourages us to bring curiosity, resilience, and creativity to the process. Yes, shaking things up is unnerving. But that's the point.

The Seder is a communal empowerment ritual based on the insight familiar in modern times under the heading: the personal is political.

Its main tool is speech—structured speech. Haggadah comes from the word "higgid" which means to tell, to expound. Pesach—the Hebrew word for Passover—is made up of "pe" and "sach" a mouth that speaks. Passover is our annual opportunity to recalibrate the usual *seder*, the default order of our lives, including habits of communication that privilege some voices over others.

A Seder must include dialogue.

The sages tell us that even if a person celebrates the holiday alone, she should direct questions to herself and listen for answers. For those who are fortunate enough to celebrate in community, Passover is our chance to move into truer, deeper dialogue with all who are hungry for a more inclusive future.

LAG B'OMER

HILLULA TO HER HEART[6]

The mullet tosses and hog roasts of my secular, southern upbringing did little to prepare me for the party I attended in Meron, a city in Northern Israel, 15 years ago today. I was a Yeshiva student in the Mir and went with my hasidic study partner, and more than 200,000 of our closest friends, to celebrate the life of R' Shimon Bar Yochai, the author of the mystical work of the Zohar, who is buried there.

We arrived by bus, well after midnight, to a massive grassy field. The sky was illuminated through the smoke and fog from bonfires and the lights of an endless caravan of busses. I looked around for the familiar sight of pickup trucks, mud wrestling, or denim overalls – there were none.

We made our way through an overflowing indoor mosh pit of men singing, whose bodies were threatening to crush the old walls from the inside, past the animals that were tied up to be slaughtered, guarded by women in tie dyed outfits dancing like they were the only ones there. Finally we arrived at an enormous pile of wood that had been doused with leftover oil and wicks from Chanukah. The Rebbe, surrounded by hundreds of fathers and their 3 year old sons waiting for their first haircuts, lit the fire with such holy and deliberate intention that it felt like the wood had waited its entire existence for this moment and was present in conscious partnership.

It was the strangest blend of things and people that I

---

[6] Originally published on May 2, 2018 by *Tikkun*

have ever seen. What brings folks from so many diverse backgrounds to celebrate, in both relatively similar and unrecognizably different ways, at the grave of a mystic on his *yahrtzeit,* or *hillula,* in jubilant reverence in a fashion that is unparalleled in all of Judaism?

Perhaps, just as R' Shimon Bar Yochai brought forth the Zohar as a reflection of his soul, Lag B'omer invites us to cultivate and tend the unique gifts and expression of Spirit each of us brings into the world. Celebrating the commonality of individuality hosts a party like no other that supports everyone being equally themselves in original ways.

The Talmud teaches us that the actions of our ancestors are a sign for their descendants – *maaseh avot, siman l'banim.*

At Jacob's initial encounter with Rachel, he arrives at a well that is covered with a stone. When Jacob sees Rachel, he rolls the stone from the mouth of the well, waters her sheep, kisses her, and begins to weep (Genesis 29:10-11). In this passage, the stone on the well acts as a seal between worlds – when it is removed, the water from the deep flows and is gathered in affirmation and blessing of new creative potential. So, too, are we able to spiritually hydrate ourselves and the world when we recognize the wellspring of our unique wisdom we are meant to uncover.

The mystics point out that the Hebrew word in the verse to "roll" – "ויגל" *(vayigal),* alludes to the two stages of the counting of the omer. *Vayigal* can be parsed into the first *33* לג *(lamed-gimel)* and the second *16* יו *(yud-vav).* According to this teaching, the counting of the omer supports us in the heavy lifting of the stone that sits on our heart, and all that blocks us from accessing the sacred waters of our unique Torah.

The Midrash observes that there are 48 mentions of wells in the Torah. The Sefas Emes teaches that these mentions of wells are an allusion to the 48 ways that we can acquire the Torah, and that each well provides access to a particular aspect of Divine wisdom. As each well opens a unique aspect of Torah, so, too, do each of us have a portal into the Divine and Her Torah.

Lag B'omer invites us to *hillula* not simply to the gravesites of our tzadikim and beloved dead, but into a pilgrimage to discover our unique gifts of sacred teaching that is inside of us, waiting to be revealed and shared.

The word "Yisrael" "ישראל" is an acronym for "There are 600,000 letters in the Torah," corresponding to the 600,000 roots of all the souls that were at the giving of the Torah.

According to the medieval scholar and mystic Nachmanides, one of God's many names is the entire Torah of the five books of Moses – from the first letter "ב" *bet* of the first word of Genesis to the last letter "ל" *lamed* of the last word of Deuteronomy. (Together, these letters combine to spell לב - *lev* – heart). Just as a Torah scroll is not considered kosher if even one letter is missing, so too is humanity considered deficient, a reflection of God and Her Torah lacking, if even one of us is not contributing our one of a kind soul teaching. Lag B'omer reminds us to turn our attention to our particular well and drink from it thirstfully.

As you approach a *hillula* of the heart this Lag B'omer, what is the stone that is covering your well? Can you taste the spiritually sweet waters within? How do you most want to feel as you drink from them? How can you share and live with them as a communal offering?

Let yourself steep, this holiday, in the possibility that you are a necessary letter in the Divine Name, that your Torah, your wisdom, your embodied knowing, and your particular approach to the mystery of all that is, is a blessing and an essential element in the optimal expression of this world.

King David, who was born and passes away on Shavuot, writes in the first psalm
כִּי אִם בְּתוֹרַת יְהוָה חֶפְצוֹ וּבְתוֹרָתוֹ יֶהְגֶּה יוֹמָם וָלָיְלָה:

If a person desires God's Torah, in one's own Torah they toil day and night. Rashi, of 11th century Troyes, France, notices the shift from God's Torah to the Torah of the individual and explains: at first it is called God's Torah, and once we work at it, it is called our own Torah.

This speaks to how the vast majority of Jews see the Torah – that Torah is a thing, but not my thing. We are not a part of the present tense proactive delivery of the Torah. Shifting from the Torah of God (a thing) to Torah that is mine, requires the uncovering of the stone and the drawing up of the water.

At the crossroads of innovation and tradition, we celebrate those who came before us by making our own contribution to the Torah of our ancestors. We're all drawing from the same well, but we access different waters.

לָכֵן / שָׂמַח לִבִּי וַיָּגֶל כְּבוֹדִי אַף־ בְּשָׂרִי - יִשְׁכֹּן לָבֶטַח

So my heart rejoices, my whole being exults (*vayigal*) and my body rests secure (Psalm 16:9).

"My flesh" בשרי has the same letters as רשבי ("R'SBY") - Rebbi Shimon Bar Yochai.

If you feel that the Torah isn't speaking in present tense, to our needs, then give her voice. Let her flow and quench the thirst of the people. Like the prophet Amos (9:11) teaches : "A time is coming—declares my Lord God—when I will send a famine upon the land: not a hunger for bread or a thirst for water, but for hearing the words of the Lord." Be her words. She needs all y'all.

SHAVUOT

TRANSGENDER AND TRANSCENDENT[7]

Transitions can be difficult. They often occupy the uncomfortable space between the given of where we were and the unknown of where we are going. Whether it's adolescence, retirement, or a change in relationship status, it takes time to reorient and get used to who we are in our current reality.

Our tradition speaks frequently to this challenge. On Shavuot we transitioned from Hebrews to Jews, individuals to a nation, and broken fragments to a healed whole. In preparation for those epic changes our ancestors transitioned incrementally, from a deep level of spiritual impurity, to being worthy of divine revelation.

Shavuot offers us reminders to be accepting of change. We celebrate the power and invitation to transcend what is given by reading the Book of Ruth, which speaks to her conversion from Moav to the Jewish People. King David, a descendant of Ruth who was born and died on Shavuot, is offered by the Talmud as the example to encourage others to transition from sin to righteousness. Even the cheese cake, a dairy product traditionally eaten on Shavuot, reminds us of the transformative change that the body goes through in order to produce milk.

Our tradition acknowledges the fluidity of the human experience in that we have the ability to affect change in ways that seem to contradict the physical by the spiritual.

---

[7]Originally published on May 26, 2017 by the Jewish Orthodox Feminist Alliance Blog, under the pen name Kol Raychaim

The sun can be shining and still we can make it Shabbos on Friday afternoon by our intent to accept and welcome it early. A person can dedicate something to the Temple, making it holy, and then redeem it back to the mundane. When we repent out of love, those sinful actions of the past are retroactively converted to merits. Traditionally, when it comes to the transition of people, time, objects, and actions, we accept, without any hesitation, the legitimacy of the change.

Change is part of life and our faith. When it comes to gender, some find it hard to acknowledge the elasticity of human identity. Some see it as fixed, with an unnatural rigidity of permanence that is completely non-malleable. The concept of transgender is too lubricious for many to grasp. In truth, it's hard for me to understand because I've never felt any tension in my own gender identity. Yet, we must listen and try to comprehend. It is part of the journey towards understanding God's wisdom.

As I have evolved I've learned that if we amputate our past identity, we risk experiencing phantom pain for life.

We, unlike God, occupy a physical and finite space. By necessity, we have a dominant expression of a limited body, but it is just a superficial shell. Below the surface we are able to see and hold all of those contradictory and mutually exclusive aspects simultaneously.

The greatness of God is displayed in that we are all equally created in the image of God, who has no physical image, and still we all look different. It is those differences that provide insight into the Divine, as they are a reflection of it. According to tradition, there are 600,000 letters in the Torah and ישראל, Yisrael, is an acronym corresponding to a head count at Mount Sinai. The individual is to the nation what a letter is to the Torah. If even one is missing, it is incomplete.

The Torah was not given to an individual, but to a nation. However, that nation was unified like one person with one heart. It is this space of holding both identities simultaneously that allows and contributes to divine revelation. I've observed that the phrase כלל ישראל כאיש אחד בלב אחד is equal in Hebrew numerology (*gematriya*) to יש הרבה דרכים למקום. "The Jewish People as one person with one heart" has the same numerical value as "there are many ways to reach God."

Exodus 20:15 testifies that the entire nation saw the sounds by the mountain. I am not synesthetic nor am I transgender, but I believe both come from an expansive awareness of areas that most can't perceive.

It was exactly at that moment of awareness that all of our souls were being reunited as one, that the artificial limitation of the body was overpowered and could no longer confine the true expression of soul. We were our truest selves in our most natural habitat; one of spirituality.

It is that perspective and sense of belonging that Judaism gives to the world: we are an infinitely beautiful and unique blend of all that which is holy and way too deep to be defined by words or pronouns. Like the seasons and corresponding festivals, there is an expressed texture to time which we experience as real in the moment but is guaranteed to change in the future.

The Torah wasn't given to just support the experience of the majority – it was intentionaly given in a way that extended beyond our lived experiences to show us how it is to be used in the future. This year, when we accept the Torah, let us do so like it was done originally - by also accepting each other.

CISGENDER HUMILITY AND ACCEPTING THE TORAH[8]

"How do you know that you are a boy?" asks the father of a trans child, knowing that the answer can't possibly be the same as his own visual confirmation of masculine identity. "I just am," answers the child. It is the simplicity of his son's response that guides the father to the realization that his own inability to perceive gender beyond the physical is exactly what make him cisgender and not trans. Sometimes, what we don't understand is much more informative than what we think we know.

The Talmud teaches "Accustom your tongue to say: I do not know," as a way of preserving credibility. We are even encouraged to frame knowing that we don't know, עד ללא ידע, as the highest level of knowledge.

Tradition highlights this through the term used for a rabbinic scholar, *talmid chacham*. "Talmid" means student and "chachum" means wise. By calling the scholar a student, it teaches us that if we don't see ourselves first as learners, then we will never be available to acquire true wisdom.

When King Ptolemy of Egypt brought together 72 elders and told them separately to translate the Torah, God inspired each of them to alter the verse, "Let us make man in Our image and in our likeness," (Genesis 1:26) to "I shall make man in an image and a likeness." The "us" in this verse is commonly interpreted as an invitation to the

---

[8] Originally published on May 16, 2018 by the Jewish Orthodox Feminist Alliance Blog

angels to participate in creation. To prevent the verse from being mistakenly read as evidence for multiple gods, God inspired the elders to translate it differently.

Rashi asks why, if the verse is so easily misunderstood, did God write it in this way to begin with? He answers that it comes to teach us to be humble even when we are confident in our knowledge of the world, by consulting with others. The deeper teaching here is that it is specifically in situations where we are forced to question our understanding of the world that we must humble ourselves in order to be open to receive truth.

Tradition teaches that this verse from Genesis alludes to a verse from Psalm 118: "The stone the builders despised has become the cornerstone." The first word of the verse, stone (אבן), serves as an acronym for the words "Let us make man." (Genesis 1:26). The Chida (18th Century Israel) says that this unwanted stone is a reference to Ruth, who many mistakenly assumed not to be Jewish because she was from Moav. Yet later in life, she is given a special seat in the Holy Temple built by her great-great-grandson, the King of Israel, Solomon. Perhaps God is inviting us to emulate God's humility and gently reminding us how wrong and unaware we really are, especially when we are arrogant.

The commentaries point out that the most beautiful stone is chosen as the cornerstone of the Temple because it can then be seen and appreciated from two sides. Similarly, the Ten Commandments were carved all the way through the two stone tablets, but miraculously appeared the same from both sides.

We read the story of Ruth on Shavuot to remind us that if we really want to be able to see, understand, and appreciate the beauty of Torah, then we need to be able to see it from the other side as well.

Moses was introduced to God by the *sneh*, the small burning bush and accepted the Torah on the lowly mountain of Sinai. It was because he was the humblest of people that he was able hold the Torah and serve as the shepherd of the Stone of Israel.

When we love someone we try to understand them and see things from the other's perspective. If we don't understand gender variations maybe we can reach out, listen, and hold the space of not knowing with humility and love.

This idea is illustrated with the following story told of Rav Meir Simcha of Dvinsk, known as the Ohr Somayach: Two Yeshiva students were struggling with a particularly difficult Talmudic commentary and approached the rabbi for help. He told the students to pause from learning and pray for more love of the Torah.

One of the students asked curiously, "Once we are going to pray, why don't we just pray for the answer to our question?" The rabbi explained that the more you love something the greater your sensitivity to and awareness of its specific needs. If we have a greater love for the Torah, then we will naturally understand it better, just as a true friend knows the needs of another.

Onkelos posits that the word stone (אבן), is an abbreviated form of the Hebrew words for father and son (אב–בן). The Talmud often reads "children" homiletically as "builders." Tradition has it that the third Temple will be built, in part, from the stones of the sacred spaces we construct, rebuilding God's house out of love.

We pray, "Return us, Father, to your Torah," and the prophet tells us that we will return through our children. There are things parents can teach their children, and clearly there are things children can teach us. If we want to receive the Torah we need to love all of God's children more than we love our false sense of knowing.

RABBINIC RESPONSIBILITY FOR LGBTQ JEWS[9]

The Jerusalem Talmud offers some life saving advice for new rabbis to see communal responsibility as spiritual practice. It opens with a very distressing statement: If someone is in a life threatening situation and the rabbi is asked if it is permissible to desecrate the Shabbos in order to try and save the person's life, it is a repulsive thing. The commentators explain that the deficiency lies in the scholars who didn't make it properly know how Judaism elevates life over ritual observance. We find even harsher language in the Code of Jewish Law (Orach Chayyim 328:2): It is a mitzvah to desecrate the Shabbos on behalf of such a person. One who does so punctiliously is praiseworthy, and one who asks if it is permissible is a murderer.

If one who asks is called murderous, what do we call those who silence the question by denying the existence of LGBTQ folks and their needs?

We can repent, if necessary, for being too zealous in creating safe spaces, but no amount of repenting will ever bring back someone that we have failed to protect. Those who deny the dignity of LGBTQ folks go against this core Jewish teaching.

As we prepare for Shavuot, and accepting the Torah, I would like to share with you what I find to be the comfort and responsibility it contributes to the world by

---

[9] Originally published on May 1, 2018 on the Congregation Beit Simchat Torah website (cbst.org)

briefly exploring the mitzvah of saving a life. In, Leviticus 18:5 we read: "You shall observe My decrees and My judgments, which a person shall carry out and live by them - I am Hashem."

On this verse Maimonides writes, "Learn that the laws of the Torah only exist in the world for mercy, loving kindness, and peace. It is the heretics who say that this (breaking the Shabbos in order to save a life) is a desecration of the Shabbos and is forbidden. It is on them that Ezekiel 20:25 writes: 'Wherefore I gave them also statutes that were not good, and ordinances whereby they could not live'." (Maimonides Mishneh Torah- Laws of Shabbos 2:3).

There is a fascinating disagreement in rabbinic literature on the Divine, pre-Sinaitic expectation of one's own spiritual practice when it is in conflict with the physical well being of another. It is worth investigating the baseline of natural law, in order to better understand the layer that the Torah adds.

God appeared to Moses in Midian and instructs him to return to Egypt and tell Pharaoh to free the Children of Israel. At the same time, Moses has a son who needs to be circumcised. The medieval commentator Rashi quotes Moses' internal conflict. "Shall I perform the circumcision and then depart on the journey? Traveling poses a danger to the infant until three days. Shall I perform the circumcision and wait three days? But, The Holy One has commanded me, 'Go! Return to Egypt'." Before the Torah was given, did the physical wellbeing of another factor into one's own spiritual calculation?

The Mizrachi (c. 1455-1526) argues that Moses is punished for not following the Divine directives to both circumcise his son and go back to Egypt. Exodus 4:24 reads "When he was on the way, at the inn, Hashem encountered him and sought to kill him" because he chose to delay the circumcision. Mizrachi explains that the verse "to live by them," which permits a person to prioritize life over fulling commandments, hadn't yet been given and therefore if God tells you to do something, it is at all cost.

The Maharal of Prague (c. 1520-1609) is very disturbed by this position and writes that we don't need the Torah to come and teach us that folks don't need to die so that others can perform better spiritually, "because there are many things that wise people know from being intuitive about rational ideas." So what then is the verse "to live by them" instructing us, if we already know that we don't need to prioritize "being observant" over another's well being, even without being told so explicitly?

When we stood under the mountain as "one person with one heart," we no longer saw another's physical needs as competing with our own spiritual ones. With this verse we are commanded to ensure that all are provided for: *Yenum's Olam HaZe is Mine Olam HaBa*, another's physical world is my spiritual world!

The Torah was never given to individuals, but only to the collective. We live in very difficult times. Religion can help. Community can help. Religious communities have a unique responsibility in preventing feelings of isolation and rejection that are the largest contributors to suicide. Situations in which there is only a small chance that it will result in a fatality, God forbid, are considered life-threatening by Jewish law and require all means necessary to try and save the person. For folks whose very identity is challenged, protested, and threatened, who say "Rabbi, you don't understand, I can't keep living like this," by not being supportive, it is we who are creating the life-threatening situation.

Accepting the Torah requires us to be outwardly focused towards those who are the most vulnerable, marginalized, and frightened. May we restore the glory and healing of God, Torah, and the Jewish People by re-embracing the holy posture of unified inclusivity just like we did at Mt. Sinai; like one person with one heart seeing the needs of others as our own.

SPEAKING ABOUT AIDS ON SHAVUOT[10]

Speech created this world and still has the ability to change it. Before God could say "let there be light" there needed to be letters to form those words.

בְּרֵאשִׁית בָּרָא אֱלֹהִים אֵת הַשָּׁמַיִם וְאֵת הָאָרֶץ

In the beginning God created א ת ; the A to Z of the Hebrew Alphabet. King David, who was born and died on Shavuot, wrote in Psalms: הֶאֱמַנְתִּי כִּי אֲדַבֵּר אֲנִי עָנִיתִי מְאֹד , "I have faith, although I say 'I suffer exceedingly'." Talking about the suffering gives everyone more faith that we can do something about it. This Sunday is the Aids Walk and the Jewish community doesn't talk enough about AIDS.

How are we meant to respond to conversations that are not even being had? God answered the silence with illuminating speech and began the process of removing the dark emptiness and void in the universe. The Midrash sees this space as God's loneliness. It's not good for us to be alone because we are created in the image of God, and it isn't good for God to be alone. God is a giver and it is painful not to be in relationship with those who can share in what we have.

We find a similar pain of temporary isolation as part of the restorative process of צרעת Tzaras (also parsed as a time of constriction עת צר), an affliction acquired by misusing speech to minimize others. It is also the same letters as עצרת atzeret, the Biblical name for Shavuot (holiday of receiving the Torah), observed this weekend. Atzeret literally means gathered and connotes joy and

---

[10] Originally written on May 18. 2018

celebration.

Sefer Yetzirah, an early mystical work articulates this spectrum: "There is nothing in goodness above delight ענג or worse than נגע affliction." Goodness is only increased when it can be shared with those we love and pain is amplified when we have no one to help support us in the struggle.

Shavuot, also means oath. With the Torah also came a commitment and responsibility to each other. The Torah was never given to an individual, only to the collective. No one person can fulfill the spiritual requirements of the 613 commandments by themselves, just as no one can successfully live in the physical world without being in community.

בְּרֵאשִׁית , Genesis is understood by Rashi as referring to the Torah itself בִּשְׁבִיל הַתּוֹרָה שֶׁנִקְרֵאת רֵאשִׁית - for the Torah that is called first. This world was created for the Torah, in that the Torah is the scaffolding to hold up the communal support we have for humanity. It is further alluded to on the 6th day of creation. יום הששי; the sixth of sivan, this Sunday, when the Torah was given.

The word "good" is found by the individual days of creation and then shifts to "very good" when all that was created comes together as a collective world. It not good for people to be alone and it is very good to be together.

We have all pledged to be in partnership with God to protect and be responsible for all of God's children. As we celebrate receiving the Torah, as one person with one heart, let's also align our hearts with those who feel alienated and afflicted.

To find out how to get more involved, please visit: talktomeabouthiv.org

THREE WEEKS

ROSH CHODESH AND RABBISPLAINING[11]

On this day, many years ago, women said no, and men didn't listen. We were overcome by a desire for greater influence and took possession of that which didn't belong to us. Our maternal ancestors resisted but we didn't pay attention. Their gold was taken without consent and formed an idol of artificially crafted divinity.

The screams of protest against modern manifestations of those idolatrous powers are still being silenced today with the same harsh consequences of the first 17th of Tamuz. The question remains: can men resist the impulse to occupy space that does not belong to them?

Discussions about women being given access to sacred spaces, whether in the context of becoming rabbis or at the Western Wall, are being had, but on men's terms. Questions are framed around "granting" or "allowing" women to have more equality, as if it is ours to give.

We may be discussing how women can gain better access to their own Judaism, but we have yet to have a more basic conversation – namely, the way men interact with women, even in mundane spaces. It is time for us to pivot inward and invite ourselves to start listening.

Our rabbis teach that women were rewarded for opposing men in the building of the golden calf and were given guardianship over Rosh Chodesh, the new moon. Each new appearance of the moon represents a faulty attempt – similar to that of the golden calf – to expand perceived power and domination over a shared space. The

---

[11] Originally published on July 11, 2017 by the Jewish Orthodox Feminist Alliance Blog

Talmud relates that the moon wasn't content with being equal to the sun and asked God, "Can two kings use the same crown?" Despite the fact that the moon is focusing on its own stature, it fails to recognize that the sun was the true source of light, and the moon only a faint reflection of it. God shrinks the moon as punishment for trying to claim dominion over what should have been a shared space.

We too reflect God's light, and are charged with recognizing that shared source in others. Each Rosh Chodesh encourages us to renew our commitment to be present with one another as equals.

This upcoming month, Av, meaning father and representing the patriarchy, is the saddest month of the year and contains the harshest decrees. But the early mystical work, Sefer Yetzirah, also teaches that Av corresponds to the act of listening. We choose to hear by developing sensitive listening practices so as not to unintentionally contribute to the climate of misogyny.

Today we experience the painful reminder that society still hasn't learned how to listen to others' experiences. It is our turn to start listening. What would need to happen for men to support spaces in which women speak first? Are we capable of accustoming ourselves not to interrupt or interject when a woman is talking? Rather than being dismissive, how can we increase our respect for women's opinions and take their ideas more seriously?

God is everywhere and there is room for everyone. But if we fill this world with just self, then there isn't space for anyone, including God. Let us accept this Rosh Chodesh Av as a restorative one. We need to break the cycle of elevating ourselves through minimizing others. The world suffers when women's voices are ignored. Are we ready to start listening?

9TH OF AV LETTER TO DAY SCHOOLS[12]

To Whom It May Concern,

I am a rabbi at Columbia University and a graduate of Beth Medrash Govoha in Lakewood, NJ. I have transgender students, transgender congregants, and I have a transgender family member.

As Jewish educators, we don't teach Torah, in that the Torah doesn't need us as a rebbe. Rather, we teach children, God's children - in God's dwelling place, the classroom.

We are taught in Shabbos 119b that God's house in Jerusalem was only destroyed because schoolchildren were diverted from learning Torah. The Maharal, 16th century Prague, observes that the purity and holiness of schoolchildren is greater than that of the Holy Temple. He explains that the wood and stones of the Temple are limited in their ability to accept holiness by their finite physical nature. By contrast, children, possessing an eternal soul, have an expansive capacity to hold God's holiness through Torah learning. When the Jewish People prevented schoolchildren from being the natural receptacle of Torah that they are, it showed that they were not sensitive enough to appreciate even the lower level holiness of the Temple, and were therefore unworthy of it.

What do our actions say about our understanding of the Torah, which doesn't itself have a soul, when we deny its intended purpose, which is to be learned by the souls of

---

[12] Originally written in September of 2016

God's children? We are only worthy to teach Torah when we can appreciate the holiness and goodness of those whom we are teaching.

All of God's children are equally loved and entitled to the inheritance of a Jewish education, because they are the holiest among us.

No child should be denied admission based on gender identity. Further, Jewish schools should be welcoming, respectful, and affirming of the gender identities expressed by students. This means at least assuring safe and comfortable bathroom access, usage of preferred pronouns, and gender-affirming application of school dress codes.

The divine mandate to teach Torah comes with the holy responsibility to teach it properly - holding in our hearts that each child's most pronounced identity is being created in the image of God.

MORAL MINCHA – PROTESTING OUTSIDE OF THE ORTHODOX UNION[13]

Growing up in Richmond, VA in the 80's, I attended a Hebrew school that put a very strong emphasis on Holocaust education. We read books, saw pictures and movies, and went to museums. They were graphic, traumatizing, and I felt very strongly at the time, age inappropriate: that so early on we should be exposed to these human atrocities. It also, thank God, felt completely un-relatable to my lived experience.

It was only now, when I was in Texas, at the border, that I felt for the first time ever an appreciation for that education. I had the most unexpected visceral reaction.

Never again isn't just a function of being able to insure that we don't forget, but it is also the ability to recognize it in order to prevent it from ever happening again!

So quickly the situation seems to be devolving into just another experience, without any sense of urgency. People are being dehumanized, monetized, and treated worse than objects. When we order something online, we know exactly where it is, and here, we are losing people because we have devalued human life. We are no longer seeing all people as people.

Separation is bad. To such an extent that in the Biblical account of creation, on the day that the waters are separated, the phrase "it was good" is omitted. Because it is not good.

---

[13] Originally delivered as a speech on July 10, 2018

The rabbis point out that when God separated the light and darkness it does say that "it was good" since those things are mutually exclusive. However water, like children, naturally cleaves to its source. When we seperate those that belong together, it is evil. It is unholy. It is unGodly.

We are living in a time of darkness that I have never seen but have only heard about. For the first time I feel a sense of gratitude to my teachers who had the wisdom to make us feel so uncomfortable through watching all of those movies and hearing the stories that seemed so removed, because now this - this feels familiar. I've seen this before. We have seen this before. This has happened before.

At the Texas border we tried to deliver books, toys, and diapers. We were denied access and our contributions were rejected. There is no excuse. We can send things to inmates in prisons, but we can't give clothing to children that we have placed in cages.

The folks there are being detained because we see them as different. As Jews, we are also different and we know better. We know that once any group of people is separated out for being "other," it is only a matter of time until we are also separated out.

We are here, protesting outside of the Orthodox Union, because we expect better. The month that we are about to enter into, Av, is the saddest month of the year. It is also intended to provide some comfort in that we are still able to see God as a parent; recognizing that the parental bond can never be broken. There is hope in that. There is compassion in that. There is mercy in that.

But what does it say about the patriarchy, about male rabbis who are supporting and honoring those who are separating children from their parents? It is the source of why this month is the saddest in the calendar. We have lost the compassion that comes when we see people as God's children.

If we can make a distinction between their children and ours, then we are not recognizing that they are all God's children.

It is for that reason that we no longer have a temple, that we no longer have God as a parent - that we can't see each other as siblings. Until this stops, the destruction will continue. This is not new. It has been going on for two thousand years. Because someone is different we deny them space at the table.

There is no way to justify, after all of the horrors that we have witnessed and endured, our recreation of another atrocity, today, in our country.

How are we going to make this 9th of Av different? How are we going to look to our leaders who have failed us by taking the power and privilege of leadership positions and have aligned themselves with the oppressors instead of being allies to those in real need of basic resources?

It was disgusting to be standing outside of a detention center in Texas, it was 104 degrees - with all of the wealth of this great nation and not be able to provide for the basic needs of these children; that we separated from their parents. An administration that has deliberately destroyed the documentation necessary to reunite these children with their parents. The only way that this can happen is when we dehumanize people. Until we can see the Godliness in each and every human, this will continue.

The rabbis who claim to have a monopoly on the truth, who want to keep that privilege and not share it, and not expand the tent - you must own these choices and decisions and answer for them. How do you hoard this power and without being overwhelmed with the guilt of not using it to help those who are truly in need? Are you just preoccupied and distracted by the selfish pursuit of acquiring more power?

It is why the month of Av, which corresponds to the tribe of Shimon and the action of hearing, is the saddest month, because if you can hear the children cry and not be called to make sure that they can be held by their parents once again - when so many of our parents and our grandparents never got to hear the cries of their children ever again – if you can align yourself with someone who is manufacturing this humanitarian crisis - how can we have faith in you as rabbis?

And so we mourn. We will mourn this Tisha B'Av like we have for the last two thousand years, since the destruction of the last temple, because nothing has changed.

We are overdue for change and we must demand that this year be different.

ROSH HASHANAH

ROSH HASHANAH: A TIME FOR DIVINE CONSENT[14]

Twenty-five years ago, when I was a teenager at orientation for Jewish summer camp, a retired doctor got up to talk about STDs and then segued into consent. To a room full of young Jewish men he said: "If a girl says 'no,' she means no. If she says 'don't,' she means don't. And if she says 'stop,' she means stop. But if she says all three together – well then there is room to negotiate."

We all laughed, unaware of how we were contributing to a climate of misogyny and violence against women. Times have changed since that talk in the pavilion, but I'm not sure how much, to be honest. Now, with twenty-five more years behind me, and with a teenage son and daughter myself, I feel that just as repentance requires a change in action, so too is there an urgent need for communal detoxing, especially from male Jewish leaders and role models

The objectification of women and the invariable violence that ensues is nothing new, unfortunately. We read the biblical narrative of Dina being raped by Shechem, and the forced beauty pageants in the time of Queen Esther. Every year before Rosh Hashanah we also read about the Eishet Yefat Toar – the woman of attractive appearance.

When a soldier went out to war and found a non-Jewish woman he desired, he was permitted to take her

---

[14] Originally published on September 6, 2018 by the Jewish Orthodox Feminist Alliance Blog

captive and she would go through a mourning process said to make her less attractive. At the conclusion of this thirty day period, the soldier was encouraged to release her, but was also given the option to marry her. The verse uses a strange word for this transitional period: "yerech," meaning month. The Zohar says this refers to the current month, Elul.

The laws of Eishet Yefat Toar are given in the context of the verse, "When you go out to war against your enemies" (Deuteronomy 21:14). The rabbis point out that the verse shouldn't need to mention "enemies." Obviously if you are going to war against them, they are by definition your enemies. Rather, the rabbis frame "enemies" here as the Yetzer Hara – our internal evil inclination. Indeed Rashi, on this verse, quotes the Talmud that "the Torah is only speaking in opposition of our evil inclination."

So what advice is the Torah offering to combat the inhumane desire to exercise dominion over women? And why is this relevant to the month of Elul in preparation for Rosh Hashanah?

The Gaon, Rabbi Elijah of Vilna (1720-1797), observes that there are two words for desire in Hebrew: "cheshek" and "chefetz." The word that is used by Shechem in the rape of Dina (Genesis 34:19), about the woman captured in war (Deuteronomy 21:14), and with Esther (2:14), is "chefetz." It is not coincidental that it is also the word used for an object. When we perceive someone only as a thing that can fulfill our desire, then we dehumanize them.

The alternative word for desire is "cheshek," an elevated way of yearning and passionate longing, the way that God does towards us (Deuteronomy 7:7) and the way we are meant to cleave to the Torah (Yevamot 63b).

Elul is the time when God created the world because God's perfection also has needs, primarily the need to give. The Ramchal, 18th century Italy, writes: "Since God alone is the true good, God's desire will be satisfied only when benefiting others." This month invites us to reflect on how God engages in relationship with people. God's intimacy is an invitation that requires active consent from another.

When God wants to be close to us through the Shabbos, God tells Moses, "I have a precious gift in my storehouse… Go and let them know" (Shabbat 10b). We do the same on Friday night when we greet the shabbat bride. We turn and face the entrance, share our intent… and wait.

Each week we say in kiddush, "And the Children of Israel guarded the Shabbos." We are reminded that things which are powerful need to be protected to make sure they are only used for good. In Hebrew, the first letter of each word spells the word for intimacy, rendering it "and they protected sacred space." It is a communal responsibility to create a world that respects all people as people.

Rosh Hashanah is the day that God created a boundary in our relationship and an expectation that we respect it. It is also the day that we didn't listen and ate from God's forbidden fruit. As unrecognizably different as the world is from that time, and my world from twenty-five years ago, the working parts unfortunately are the same, and the quest to honor the rights of others continues.

This year again has seen the horrific dehumanization of people in our country: children torn from their parent's arms at the border and put in cages, people of color afraid that just living could cost them their lives, women continuing to be objectified, harassed, and abused, and a bill in Massachusetts this November that would legalize discrimination against transgender folks in public places if passed.

These atrocities are only possible when we fail to see all people as equally created by the Divine, but rather as a "chefetz" – an object that can be exploited or disposed of if it doesn't align with the vision of those with power.

These policies are moving quickly and in worse directions.

How can those of us with the privilege of our voices being heard raise them more powerfully on behalf of those whose needs and rights are being violated? What can we do to amplify the screams of those in the world that protest "No, I am not okay with this!"

With each blast of the shofar, envisioning the cries of those still oppressed, let us realign ourselves with God and model the practice of active consent, combat efforts to dehumanize people, and commit to the unrelenting struggle to fulfill the holy desire of a world where all are free, safe, and respected.

COMING OF AGE AS GENDER NON-CONFORMING[15]

In the Shema we read: "וְשִׁנַּנְתָּם לְבָנֶיךָ וְדִבַּרְתָּ בָּם," "Teach them to your children and speak with them." "Them" (בם) has been understood as an acronym for the first word of Genesis, "בראשית" and of the opening mishnah of the Talmud, "מתי" (when). The word "מתי" comes from the Mishnah's opening question, when do we begin reciting the Shema of the evening? Together, these words stand for the entire written and oral law.

Part of the lesson we are meant to impart to children is that whenever we start something new, there is a desire to ask "when will we get there." On the journey of Rabbinic Allyship for gender nonconforming b'nai mitzvah, we are just getting started.

Everyday, as cis-clergy at Congregation Beit Simchat Torah, the largest LGBTQ synagogue in the world, we think about what it means to identify as a woman or as a man, and about how to continue becoming the people we aspire to be, culturally, socially, and spiritually. Serving CBST means that we are frequently asked to provide language and guidance for gender non-conforming kids who are looking for a ritual that supports who they are, rather than forcing them into the binary of either bar or bat mitzvah (son or daughter of the commandments).

How can we structure this ancient rite of passage so

---

[15] Originally published on August 30, 2018 by the Jewish Orthodox Feminist Alliance Blog, co-authored with Rabbi Yael Rapport

that it inspires children to transition into Jewish adulthood, while also being sensitive to the struggles they face in a community that does not provide gender affirming language beyond the binary?

The Vilna Gaon posits that the first mishnah is focused on Shema because when a child becomes an adult at sundown, it will be the first biblical commandment for which they are responsible. As adults, when we find ourselves in uncharted territory, the Shema continues to be a helpful tool. It offers navigational advice for the new traveler asking, "Are we there yet?" or "When will we finally achieve social change?"

No one knows where or how long our path goes, and all we can do is reach for the best in each moment. For us all that means: קורין את שמע, read the Shema, because whoever we are, wherever we find ourselves, we seek to be grounded in our connection to God, who is everywhere at all times.

We believe the Torah contains the details that are important in our relationship with God. The time of a b'nai mitzvah is when God says that we are mature enough to take responsibility for our own unique and intimate relationship with God. It is when we've reached the age of consent, and know enough about who we are and how we should be behaving to be held accountable for our choices.

The Shema invites us to connect with God not just through an aspect of our identity, but rather to love God with all of our heart, with all of our soul, and with all of our might. These words have been the last ones spoken for millions of our ancestors as they left this world to be reunited with their Creator, no longer in need of a physical body. The Shema itself testifies that Israel heard, was present, and connected with God, all in one moment. When we say it we are meant to unify and become one with The One. Thus, the union that occurs during the Shema is one that allows us to transcend the needs of the physical body.

Rosh Chodesh Elul, the day that Moses ascended the mountain to receive the second set of tablets, is a month designated for self reflection on where we are in our relationship with God, and what course corrections may be necessary for us to return to our true selves.

The verse in Song of Songs, אני לדודי ודודי לי, "I am my beloved's and my beloved is mine" (6:3), alludes to this closeness by spelling the name of the month, Elul, with the first letter of each word. It additionally reminds us that we must first acknowledge ourselves as individuals before we ask someone else to accept us for who we are.

In the mystical work of Sefer Yetzirah, Elul is ruled by the letter "י" and corresponds to מעשה, action. Our patriarch, Jacob, was proactive in taking this letter from his brother as they struggled in the womb. Esav (עשו), meaning complete, should have a "י" at the end to spell out "עשוי," and Yaakov (יעקב) means heel (עקב) and does not need a "י" at the beginning. The Genesis verse hints that the struggle was over this letter: וְאַחֲרֵי כֵן יָצָא אָחִיו וְיָדוֹ אֹחֶזֶת בַּעֲקֵב עֵשָׂו. The Midrash reads "וְיָדוֹ" as a "י," rendering the verse: And then, this brother emerged grasping his "י."

The Zohar teaches that the consequences of the struggle are also reflected in the calendar in that Esav dominates the destructive and mournful three weeks leading up to Tisha B'av, while Jacob reigns over the contemplative month of Elul. As children of Israel, we respond to the Shema's call for individualized presence in personal relationship with God. This moment of exploration can be thought of as providing a religious framework for those struggling with gender identity.

The Slonimer Rebbe teaches that the evil of Esav comes from the false sense of being fully formed and complete, believing there is no further need for transformation. By contrast, Jacob's holiness comes from the constant commitment to growth and self-actualization. His life is one of continuous transition and evolution, modeling for us how to embrace many identities.

All beginnings, every change, starts with recognizing that something is missing and we want to do something about it. This month invites us to also recreate ourselves, in the most authentic, embodied way.

Our permanent identity is as a child of God, including and directly as a result of our many, varied forms of gender identity and expression. As we approach Rosh Hashanah, where we revisit the creation and the blessing of all things, we recognize it also as the day that the original, primordial "Adam" transitioned to a new expression of man and woman.

If cisgender folks would be as conscious and deliberate with our religious identities as trans and gender non-conforming people are with theirs, there would be no question about Jewish continuity. Holiness is achieved only through unrelenting struggle, and becoming a Jewish adult comes with the acknowledgment that not everything that we observe is acceptable. There are many voids that need to be filled, wounds that need to be healed, and eternal truths applied to a changing world.

As a new year approaches and our world continues its own ongoing transition, we are reminded that we each have unique roles to play, and a great deal to learn about ourselves and each other. As rabbis we teach students, and our students have a lot to teach us as rabbis. As you come forward to take on a new mitzvah for the first time, as the community elevates you and brings you into relationship with Torah, how would you like to be called?

NEW YEARS RESOLUTION[16]

As we acknowledge another year lived and commit to resolutions for the year to come, it's a time to reflect on how we can refine our roles as allies, and help improve the lives of others.

Trans lives matter. They matter a lot. They matter to parents of trans children, to children of trans parents, to brothers and sisters of trans siblings, to friends and colleagues in every part of the workforce, military, and community. And most of all, they matter to God , in whose image they are created and whose holiness they reflect.

Kavod ha'briyot - honoring God's creations with dignity - is such a powerful principle in Judaism that the Talmud says it overrides almost all other biblical commandments. But as a people, we haven't honored that commitment: to provide basic equality and respect for so many of God's children.

Trans lives matter. The lives they live matter. We are all responsible not just to protect the lives of each other, but also to defend the quality of those lives. The attempted suicide rate for trans folks, not accepted by the people closest to them, is over 40% and the average life expectancy of a trans women of color in this country is just 35 years old.

While the halachic arguments for trans equality based on pikuach nefesh, saving a life, are tragically real, we must

---

[16] Originally published on January 7, 2019 as a video on Congregation Beit Simchat Torah's Facebook page

also elevate our awareness of the Torah's obligation to be allies to honor the trans experience and assure the dignity of trans folks in daily living.

Working to stop violence, murder, and suicide, God forbid, is just not enough. We wouldn't want to live just on the other side of that line, and neither should our neighbors.

The constant fear and anxiety that trans individuals experience at airports, in bathrooms, and even in synagogues on a daily basis can no longer be tolerated... It's absolutely unacceptable that anyone should have to live under the constant threat of discrimination or hate for just being. We must own it and do everything we can to fix it.

The Mishnah teaches, "Who is an honorable person? One who honors others, as it says in the Prophets 'for those who honor God, God will honor'."

Rav Chaim Volozhin explains the proof text and offers a simple approach to integrate this teaching into our daily lives.

He writes: If we honor all people we don't engage in an internal discernment of who is worthy or if folks are better than we are, but rather remind ourselves, in our hearts, that everyone is created in the image of God, and created by God. When we honor people we honor God, and then we are worthy of God's honor.

Trans lives matter, so let's help create a world in which we can all thrive. We can't just be supportive so that folks stop dying, but must continue working until everyone can truly live.

EXPANDING THE "WE" FOR ROSH HASHANAH[17]

When we bless God before participating in mitzvah, even those that seem highly individualized like netilat yadayim, the sanctified washing of our hands, we do so as part of a collective. The blessing we recite beforehand declares, "who sanctifies **us** with God's commandments." Similarly, when we confess our sins, as we will be doing in just a few days, it is also in the plural: "**our** Father, **our** King, **we** have sinned before you." There is holiness in the collective, and we must consider each other as we repent, and repent for having not considered each other enough.

As we prepare for Rosh Hashanah, the day when the entire world is judged, we are called to reflect upon not just ourselves, but on our community as a whole. Who have we lifted up? Who have we forsaken? Often, we create our community by separating the "us" from the "them." How might the world be different if we expanded the "we" to the world; we who are created by God? What blessings might be actualized if we worked to fulfill the words of our own prayers?

This week, like every Shabbos before Rosh Hashanah, we begin the Torah reading with the following words:

אַתֶּם נִצָּבִים הַיּוֹם כֻּלְּכֶם לִפְנֵי יְהוָה אֱלֹהֵיכֶם

You stand this day, all of you, before the Lord your

---

[17] Originally published on September 9, 2018 by Hitoreri: An Orthodox Movement for Social Change, co-authored with Rebecca Krevat

God (Deuteronomy 29:9).

What was special about that day? Are we not always before God?

Rashi contextualizes this event and explains this day as Rosh Hashanah, the day we became responsible for each other.

YOU ARE STANDING THIS DAY—"This teaches that Moses assembled them in the presence of the Omnipresent on the day of his death, in order to initiate them into a covenant with God."

Tradition teaches that the covenant being referred to here is the covenant of of arvut, of being guarantors for each other, that we committed to on that day. As guarantors we protect and care for each other. We feel the responsibility to provide for each other they way we fight for our own self-preservation. The Torah was never given only to an individual or even the rabbis, but to all of us as a collective—as one person with one heart. No one person has all 613 commandments to themselves. We need each other to do the mitzvot to be complete in our relationship with God.

The Talmud (Yoma 86b) extends the breadth of our interconnectivity by explaining that the entire world is forgiven on account of a single repentant individual:

תניא היה ר"מ אומר גדולה תשובה שבשביל יחיד שעשה תשובה מוחלין לכל העולם כולו

It was taught in a Baraita that Rabbi Meir would say: Great is repentance because the entire world is forgiven on account of one individual who repents.

When we do teshuva—our acts of repentance will have a ripple effect that extends beyond the walls of our synagogues, and into the world.

Furthermore, R' Menachem Azariah of Pano (the Rama MiPano), explains that the covenant of arvut means that the soul of every other person on Earth is contained within our own soul as well. When we repent for ourselves, we are also literally repenting for each other.

The word arvut means mixture, reiterating the fact that we are all in this together. If one of us is oppressed, then we all must feel like we are the one being oppressed, because part of our soul truly is. We must feel, for example, the pain of the parent that has had their child forcefully taken at the border, on a soul level. We must open ourselves to the anxiety that trans folks experience knowing that Massachusetts will vote on whether to legalize discrimination against them because their pain is ours, and more importantly, we are responsible to do something about it.

We are now standing in divisive times where it is more urgent than ever to see the Godliness that resides within every person. We must see that our communal actions of teshuva stand as guarantors to protect each other within our community, but also that our cries for forgiveness and redemption stand to protect the entire world, our extended national and global community under God. If we want to successfully stand in front of God this Rosh Hashanah, we must see the needs of all of God's creations as our own spiritual and collective responsibility.

EDUCATING THE YATED[18]

Last night I read an article in the Yated, an Orthodox newspaper, that is very critical of my work in trans advocacy and LGBTQ inclusivity. It is indeed a *chashuvah madregah*, important state of being, to know what we don't know: *od d'lo yada*. But it is the author that demonstrated his lack of sufficient knowledge by saying that I argue for the permissibility of crossdressing in illicit relationships.

Gender identity and sexual identity are not the same thing. Who one wants to sleep with, is not the same thing as who one goes to sleep as. A person who is asexual is not genderless. Children are often aware of gender identity and completely unaware of sexual identity.

Had the author read my articles, as opposed to just quoting some of the titles, he too would have known this. You can't *pasken* a *shaylah* until you know the *metzius*. You can't answer a question if you don't know the facts - for if don't know the reality of the person who is making an inquiry, how can you properly address them. We aren't meant to answer questions, we are meant to answer people.

If a Yeshiva student asks you if he should marry a woman that he isn't attracted to, is it reasonable to tell him that it will be okay and he should go ahead and marry her? Does that answer change if he says it's not just her but all women?

No one's life is ever hypothetical. Every day I

---

[18] Originally published on August 9, 2018 as a video on the author's Facebook page

respond to the catastrophic consequences of this rabbinic malpractice. For the *lashon ha-ra* and *motzi shem ra* written and spoken about me, I am *mochel*, (I forgive the ill-intended and false statements). But for the Jewish children who were in Beit Yaakovs and Yeshiva's, but because they have two mommies or two tatties were forced out, and will now be eating pork on Yom Kippur, I can not be *mochel*.

Equally, we must all answer the same question: "What does God want from me, the result of my unique experience, now?" *Ein atah eleh teshuva*, now is the time for repentance. As a religious community we also need to make amends. Do we want to be welcoming of frum Jews who happen to be attracted to folks of the same gender, or do we want to purge the frum community from everyone who isn't cisgender and straight?

To LGBTQ Jews, especially to those who feel like this world is too much for you, you are not alone. God does not make mistakes. God does not put extra people in this world. We need you. God loves you more than anyone ever could. Don't give up on your religious identity. No one has the power to take away your relationship with God. It does get better.

As we enter Elul and ask for God to be merciful and forgiving as a parent is, let us be reminded that we must first treat each other as siblings.

SUKKOT

SUKKOT, SECURITY, AND TRANSGENDER RIGHTS[19]

Once a year we leave the safety and privilege of our homes and assume a posture of fragility by dwelling in a temporary, exposed, and vulnerable structure – the sukkah. We do this to remember what it was like to live that way. But every day, trans folks throughout the country are faced with this kind of vulnerability as their daily reality in locations without state legal protections.

In Massachusetts, there is a referendum on this November's ballot that could roll back essential legal protections. In 2016, the state legislature passed non-discrimination protections for transgender people in public spaces—any place we are when not at home, work, or school. Anyone voting in Massachusetts this November should VOTE YES to uphold these protections and ensure everyone is treated fairly.

The Torah explains the reason for sitting in a sukkah is: "So that your generations will know that I provided booths to dwell in when I took them from the land of Egypt" (Leviticus 23:43). Although we don't all live in Massachusetts, this passage and the holiday of Sukkot remind us that we were all discriminated against in Egypt, that we were provided for, and as a people are obligated to fight against discrimination everywhere.

The Torah instructs us to dwell in a sukkah. The Talmud understands that the verse in Leviticus (23:42) states it in the singular in order to teach us that one sukkah

---

[19] Originally published on September 18, 2018 by the Keshet Blog, co-authored with Seth M. Marnin

is enough for everyone. It implies that a sukkah that is not inclusive for all of us is a sukkah that is not fit for any of us.

There are three statements in the Torah that speak to a biblical expectation to sit in a sukkah (see Leviticus 23:42-43). The Vilna Gaon points out that these represent three stages in conscious inclusivity and reference Abraham's fulfillment of them, "to sit," "to dwell," and "to know."

A sukkah also has three options for the construction of its walls. It can have 4 full walls, 3 full walls, or 2 full and part of another. This is alluded to in the Hebrew word for sukkah "סכה", whose letters are formed with 4, 3, and 2.5 lines. It demonstrates that a holy space is one that is made out of different paths. A holy space is not made of just parallel lines, but of a connection with others, going in different directions. It is an open, inclusive, and inviting space like the letter "ה", hey, itself.

The Talmud teaches that this world was created with the letter "hey," which is open on the bottom and on one side. It shows that we have the freedom of movement and no one is meant to be denied entry.

The proof text is offered from Genesis 2:4 where the word for "creating [earth]," "בהבראם," is parsed as ב – with, ה -the letter "hey," ברא – [it was] created. It is also the same letters as the phrase "for Abraham," meaning that this world was created for Abraham, whose tent was open on all sides to make sure that everyone felt invited and welcomed, regardless of from where they were coming. The letter "hey" in the Torah scroll here is written smaller than usual, an allusion to the tradition that the "hey" was added later by God.

One can "sit" in a sukkah, "feel comfortable there," or reach a level to "know," that just as God protected us when we were threatened in the desert, so too must we recognize our responsibility to fight for the protection of those being dehumanized now.

So this November, please join us in voting YES on 3 in order to uphold dignity and respect for transgender people – in Massachusetts and beyond.

THE CLOUD OF GLORY[20]

Breath. When a baby is born, a child falls, or a person is dehumanized, we wait for it in that unnatural silence. We wait for the imminent scream—that hasn't yet found itself—to protest the trauma. The shock is so overwhelming that it distracts from even the unconscious act of breathing. What might it look like for us to provide the air for those gasping and to surround them with a loving cushion of it?

Tradition teaches that a "cloud of glory" accompanied the Jewish people in the desert and provided comfort and cover through their treacherous trek. Where do clouds of glory come from, and how can we access their power today to shield the vulnerable and exposed?

The mystics hint that the "cloud of glory" has its source in the human breath. With that first Divine exhale, into the nostrils of Adam, came life. After the exodus from Egypt, we finally gave it visible expression when we breathed a collective sigh of relief. We were free and held a safe space for each and every person to embrace that freedom and bond through a commonality of individuality. So precious was our united spirit that God preserved and condensed that communal breath into the form of a cloud—the cloud of glory. God is glorified when we show honor and dignity to all those who breathe.

The verse that provides the invitation to be happy on Sukkot—"You shall rejoice on your festival"—was part of

---

[20] Originally published on October 4, 2017 by the Keshet Blog, under the pen name Kol Raychaim

the covenant of communal responsibility that was given at Mount Gerizim and Ebal. The cloud of glory, the Talmud tells us, was given in the merit of Aaron, the great lover of people and peace. When the Jewish people sinned with the golden calf, there was a breakdown of the cloud. It was only when people came together in the rebuilding of that communal safe space, in the form of the mishkan (tabernacle) on the 15th of Tishrei, that our cloud of glory was reformed.

The cloud of glory necessitates total inclusion; God's breath is never wasted by putting extra people in this world. The biblical sukkah invites everyone to sit together in one dwelling place. Our happiness in the festival can't be completely achieved if there are people on the outside still looking for shelter and sanctuary.

This Sukkot, I encourage every person in the Jewish community to sign on to Keshet's Kavod Achshav | Dignity Now campaign for trans youth. By proudly declaring "Trans Jews belong here," we are partnering with God to hold all of God's children in a loving cloud of glory and safety.

CHANUKAH

WHAT DO YOU WANT YOUR CANDLE TO BE?[21]

It feels a little awkward and uncomfortable to be celebrating the miracle of light when there is so much darkness. No one's experience is ever hypothetical. I received a text from a transgender student of mine at Columbia a couple of weeks ago during finals. He was struggling with life in ways that no one ever should. What is our response to that? How do we own that communally? Fear, hate, and discrimination deny the soul spiritual expression. How can we be present and mindful of both?

Perhaps the real miracle of Chanukah is being able to see the darkness as a call and obligation to banish it with light. That is how God answered the original darkness. God said, "Let there be light" (*yehi or*). The word "yehi" (let there be) has the numerical value of 25. The original light was created on the 25th of Elul, just as on the 25th of Kislev, the Divine light was reignited, lasting eight days.

The Shelah, R' Isaiah Horowitz, 1555-1630 Prague, writes that the 36 candles we light over the course of Chanukah correspond to the 36 hours we communed with God in the Garden. Our tradition teaches that part of the original light was separated out for the righteous. So too, the light of our Chanukah candle is holy and can't be used for the mundane; its purpose is just to be. They invite us to reflect on our capacity to provide a safe space for others to be.

---

[21] Originally delivered as a drashah on December 27, 2016 at the Old Broadway Synagogue

Each one of our different and holy souls is a candle for God, as the verse in Proverbs teaches, נֵר יְהוָה נִשְׁמַת אָדָם (20:27). So we need to ask ourselves: what do I want my candle to be? Where in the darkness will I shine light? Will it be hidden in the shadows, the closet, in small groups of like minded people? Or "al pesach baiso m'bechutz," out in the streets to publicly declare to the world that the light that was, is, and will always be.

How much precarity can I take on in pushing back against those powerful sources of darkness? To what extent will I sacrifice my comfort to comfort those truly afflicted? Is my faith in the power of that Divine light strong enough to put it out there and let it be?

I've been struggling with this throughout the last year more than I've struggled in the previous 20 years combined. What do I want my candle to be?

Before I had a chance to respond to the student, the following text came through: "I'm really appreciating your existence." That is what I want my candle to be. A light to those who feel alone in the darkness. The truth is, that God is everywhere all of the time. Darkness isn't real, it is just the absence of light, and we are that light.

As a rabbi, I want to help empower people to take ownership of their unique relationship with God. How can that relationship be real or meaningful if we don't create space for people to be? It's the holiest among us that are often the most vulnerable, because their light is the brightest. To such an extent that some aren't even aware that darkness exists. Are we going to protect that light?

For me, the Chanukah candles represent the strength and sacrifices of all of those brave souls who came before us, risking everything to make it easier for us to do the same. In the Jewish tradition, we remember a person's life after they pass away though the lighting of a candle. What do you want your candle to be? It is God's light that fear, hate, and discrimination want to extinguish and it is God's light that we must defend and celebrate.

BUILDING A TEMPLE FROM TEARS[22]

The Torah is filled with instructions for building the Mishkan, God's "dwelling place" that our ancestors carried in the wilderness, but those blueprints don't provide measurements of the emotional dimensions needed to build that holy space within our hearts. It often feels like the walls we have constructed, to protect that space, are more permanent than the walls of the original Mishkan, designed to create an inviting space.

There are few things that penetrate our hearts more powerfully than the wailing cries of a child. We hear and witness the holy purity and unfiltered truth of their experience in real time. It is this portal into the honest rawness and exposed feelings of human vulnerability that naturally move us to open up our own emotional channels.

Tears can be powerful, cleansing, and soulful. They can also be the result of overwhelming pain. Regardless of the part of us that hurts, it is the eyes that cry. No other part of our body is as sensitive to the basic material of the physical world. Even one speck of dirt in the eye can be excruciating and incapacitating, where it would go completely unnoticed nearly everywhere else on the body.

Our Rabbis teach that we come into this world crying because the soul feels the pain of just being forced into this physical and constrained space of a body. Crying, it seems, is also a bridge back to that spiritual habitat.

The Talmud teaches that although the gates of prayer

---

[22] Originally published on December 9, 2018 by the Bayit Builder's Blog

are sometimes shut, the gates of tears are never closed. If so, asks the Kotzker Rebbe, 19th century Poland, why then do they need gates at all? He answers that only true, heartfelt tears are let in. It is not coincidental that the Hebrew word for crying (בכי) has the same numerical value as the word for heart (לב).

If so, why didn't Jacob cry with his son Joseph, when they are finally reunited? The verse, in this week's Torah portion (Genesis 46:29), observes that "Joseph harnessed his chariot and went to Goshen to meet his father Israel, and he appeared to him, fell on his neck, and he wept on his neck excessively." Rashi comments that while Joseph wept greatly, continuously, and more than usual – Jacob however, did not fall upon Joseph's neck nor did he kiss him but instead said the Shema.

When we recite the Shema, we close our eyes and give testimony to our faith and total commitment to the One that we can't see, but know to be the source of it all.
שמע ישראל ה' אלהינו ה' אחד

In the Torah scroll, the last letter of both the first and last word of the opening Shema phrase are trafitionally written in an enlarged manner. The large "ע" and "ד" spell the words for "witness" and "knowledge." Saying the Shema is a demonstration of our inner truth and willingness to serve God "with all of our heart, with all of our soul, and with all of our might."

Additionally, the six letters that make up the first and last words of Shema's opening phrase are an acronym for six people who sacrificed their lives in the service of God, and were miraculously saved. These two words are also acronyms for the six different literal sacrifices that were offered in the Temple, often compared to the neck, where we are told heaven and earth are connected.

Perhaps Jacob's absence of tears wasn't a denial of a shared experience with his son, but rather an expression of it.

The verse can be read as "Shema Yisrael," "Israel

(Jacob) heard": he listened, he internalized, and he responded with a complete focus of reunification with the ultimate source of goodness, healing, and power. This is one of the interpretations of Chanukah - "חנוכה" an application (חנו) of the 25 (כה) letters of the Shema.

The Greeks wanted to darken the eyes of the Jewish people. In response the Maccabees rededicate the Temple and brought forth miraculous light. The Midrash teaches that God told Israel that once the Temple is destroyed, God will desire that we say the Shema, twice a day, and it will be an elevation greater than the sacrifices themselves. That's the path that Jacob models here: eyes closed, heart open.

The temple for our soul, our Rabbis teach, is in our eyes. This is perhaps why our tradition instructs us to close the eyes of a person, once their soul has returned to its source. However, as long as our heart beats, it must beat for the collective, to see the pain of another's, as our own.

Too often we limit our vision of what we see as possible. When we connect and partner with the Omnipresent (המקום), not only is there comfort but there is a true sense of empowerment. When we look out into the world, whether our heart feels moved to tears or not, we must feel the responsibility to each other, and be willing to make an offering, because of our relationship with God.

Today is Rosh Chodesh Teves, the day tradition has it that Jacob is buried. It is also the month that is ruled by the letter "ע" and the power of a deeper sight. We must constantly rededicate our temple, allowing our soul to hear, granting it permission to cry, and letting our tears flow to form a path forward to soothe the pain of all of God's children.

COMING TOGETHER AGAINST HATE[23]

There is nothing new under the sun. As Rabbis at the world's largest LGBTQ synagogue, we have seen hate, discrimination, and anti-semitism all too frequently. It's in the space above the sun, in the spiritual place of unity, where we are able to create something new.

During the Chanukah story, when we fought for our right to keep our own identities and religious freedoms against the evil of hyper-nationalism, we rose above the physical limitations of that darkness and hate by tapping into the miraculous power of love, acceptance, and faithful optimism. We must respond now, like then, with a new commitment to increase the light as the way to dispel the darkness. Each day of Chanukah we add a candle to show that we ascend towards holiness, and are never complacent with the progress of yesterday.

The special prayer that was offered during this holiday, Psalm 30:2, models a timeless perspective on how we should respond to hate that wants to erase us out of existence. "I will exalt you, God, for You have drawn me up, and have not allowed my enemies to rejoice over me." The word in Hebrew to "draw up" is actually a contranym, meaning it has two opposite definitions, both to lower and to elevate. Just as the process of drawing water from a well first requires lowering an empty bucket, in order for it to be filled, so too the darkness is actually the process for the

---

[23] Originally published on December 10, 2018 as "Antisemitism and LGBTQ+ Hate Are Spiking – So We Must Come Together" by *OUT,* co-authored with Rabbi Sharon Kleinbaum

light, in that it obligates us to respond with a posture of creative production to be the light.

In these difficult times, we can already see the blessings that have come from our need to elevate each other. After the massacre in Pittsburgh, we saw an unprecedented amount of love and support. Our friends and neighbors, across all faith traditions, showed up for us across the country with actions of support and solidarity. Relationships within and between communities were strengthened and expanded as we came together with a unified voice of love over hate.

On Chanukah we give thanks and praise for our ability to continue holding all of our identities — without contradiction. In our tradition, the word "thanks" also means acknowledgement. We are so thankful to live in this great country that has provided support, protection, and freedoms for so many. We also acknowledge that all of this is being threatened and the fight for total equality is far from over.

The entrance to our synagogue reads, "It is good to give thanks to God ... to relate Your kindness by day and Your faith in the nights." When things seem good and clear, like day, we can speak of the kindness that we experience. When we feel the darkness, even during the day, we speak from a perspective of faith because the goodness hasn't been actualized yet. On a deeper level, we affirm our belief that God has faith in us to do something about it.

When we come out and shine our truth to the world, we are a light. When we help make it safe for others to do the same, we allow the light to spread. And when we all come together, appreciating the uniqueness of each candle, we become a light so powerful that space for hate no longer exists.

We must not be discouraged by the current rise of anti-semitism, islamophobia, white supremacy, homophobia, and transphobia. Rather, now is the time to be motivated, inspired, and empowered to stand up, more proudly than ever, with our brothers, sisters, and siblings embracing the commonality of individuality.

We are thankful for decent people of all faiths, and good conscience, who elevate humanity above differences. In this, the darkest time of the year, and the anniversary of pivotal moment in our nation's history, may we draw strength, joy, and clarity from the resistance of all those who have come before us and led by example.

Darkness isn't just the absence of light, but a call to be the light that will dispel it. It is the container that stores the most precious light, until we uncover it and let it shine through us. When we can see all people as the holy and irreplaceable candles of God, we will finally experience a true Festival of Lights.

SHEVAT

ROSH CHODESH SHEVAT AND DACA[24]

Today is Rosh Chodesh Shevat and I am out protesting the atrocious arrogance and blatant hatred that is the root of evil, ungodliness, and this administration's policy towards DACA. The cycle of the moon, the Talmud teaches, comes from its desire to be the exclusive governing luminary in the sky, completely lacking the awareness that it isn't the actual source of any light. The consequence is that it is diminished as a reminder that its light is but a reflection of the sun. So too are we a reflection of the Divine light and we are clearly in need of a reminder of our source.

Elijah the prophet is sent to rebuke a haughty rabbinical student who thinks too highly of himself. The prophet presents as someone with a very different appearance and greets the man with pleasantries. "Shalom aleichem rebbe." says the man. The student responds "Empty one! How ugly you are! Is everyone in your town this ugly?!" The prophetic voice answering the aspiring rabbi, and providing us with a timeless perspective, says "I do not know, but you should go to the Artisan that made me and say 'How ugly is the vessel you made!'."

When we can't see the Divine image in another, all we see is an empty shell. Breaking up families, separating children from parents, and the ways the repeal of DACA prioritizes ethnicity and place of birth above character, communal contributions, and life experience.

Today could be the Rosh Hashanah for the trees,

---

[24] Originally written on Jaunary 18, 2018

instead of the 15th (Tu B'Shevat), but its not. In fact, it's the only new year that isn't on the first of the month. On the first Rosh Hashanah, the day that Adam and Eve were formed, the verse teaches וַתֹּאמֶר הָאִשָּׁה הַנָּחָשׁ הִשִּׁיאַנִי וָאֹכֵל, "The serpent deceived me, and I ate." The mystics observe that the word for deception is constructed from the words "יש אני" "there is, I." Our distorted elevation of self corrupts reality and allows us to be deceived. God is truth and in those spaces of artificial inflation, hubris, and false occupation, we push God out.

In the early mystical work *Sefer Yetzirah/The Book of Creation*, the author associates the דלי, *d'li*, with this month of Shevat. A *d'li* is literally a bucket, the sign of Aquarius in the zodiac, and is related to the hebrew letter "ד" dalet, also the word for "door." It speaks to drawing up the impoverished and creating entrances leading them to better spaces. Due to Adam and Eve's selfish posture of consumption, the letter "ד" was defiled and removed from God's names of שד-י and אד"ני leaving אני, "I," and יש, "there is."

In the first mishnah of Rosh Hashanah, we learn of a dispute between the houses of Shammai and Hillel as to when the birthday of the trees is. Beit Shammai says it is today, the first of Shevat. Beit Hillel argues and posits that the new year of the trees is on the full moon, the 15th, otherwise known as Tu B'Shevat. Shammai's house of study was exclusionary, elitist, and Shammai himself famously denied entry into Judaism to potential converts. The Talmud relates that after Hillel, the radically humble and inclusive lover of humans, converted these individuals they met up and they said "Shammai's rigidity sought to drive us from the world; Hillel's humility brought us beneath the wings of the Divine Presence."

The Kabbalists teach that Shammai is punished for his policy of exclusivity by being reincarnated as Shimon ben Azzi. Shimon, in Hebrew שמעון, is actually a contraction and alludes to the sin, עון, of Shammai שם.

Hillel provides perspective on balancing solo and communal responsibility with spiritual practice. If I am not for myself, who will be for me? But if I am only for myself, what am I?

Tradition teaches that "אני" , *ani* – I, is an allusion to God, identified with the first word of the Ten Commandments. In Tractate Sukkah, Hillel teaches " אם אני כאן הכל כאן, ואם איני כאן מי כאן" "If I am here, everyone is here; and if I am not here, who is here?" If we see the Godliness of people, then everyone is welcome, but if not, it doesn't matter who is is granted entry, God won't be there.

Hillel reunited the "ד" back with the "אני" making God's name אדנ-י whole again; הלל, Hillel has the same numerical value as אדנ-י. Today, as many take a stand in support of DACA, we have an opportunity to use our privilege and democracy to take the "לי" "me" and restore the wholeness of the Divine by committing our own "ד" to make a דלי, an instrument of elevation and inclusivity.

May we heed the words of the prophet Elijah and be the vessel that God intended. Let us ally together to highlight the souls of the hundreds of thousands that are not being seen for who they are simply because of their immigration status; one of a kind, handmade, irreplaceable creations, a self-portrait of a unique aspect of God.

RENEWAL AND REBIRTH[25]

I've recently had to transition out of a position where I could provide spiritual shade, shelter, and sustenance for many of God's children who have been denied sanctuary elsewhere. Today I exist uprooted, forsaken, and rejected. It's the middle of the winter and the trees are barren. They look like they could blow over in the snowstorm. I feel like these trees look, worried that the best days are behind me with my contribution to the world decomposing on the ground. How can we be asked to celebrate the birthday of the trees when they look like they are dying and should be eulogized?

The first mishnah of Tractate Rosh Hashanah teaches that there are actually four "Rosh Hashanahs": one for the kings, one for tithings, one for years, and one for the tree. The 'tree' stands alone — it's the only one that is taught in the singular and the only one that does not fall on the first of the Jewish month, but rather the 15th (Tu B'Shevat).

Fifteen, in the Jewish tradition, resonates fullness and blooming. There are 15 individual generations that descend from Abraham to King Solomon which parallel the waxing of the moon towards its fullest reflection of divine light. The Talmud compares us to the moon, having our source of light being God instead of the sun. There are fifteen years that all three of the lives of our forefathers overlapped. We find fifteen steps in the Haggadah that we

---

[25] Originally published on February 10, 2017 as "Reflections from an Orthodox Rabbi Shunned for Being LGBTQ-Friendly" by the Keshet blog, under the pen name Kol Raychaim

read on the 15th of the month of Nissan corresponding to the 15 steps in the temple that the Levites would climb while singing 15 Shir Hama'alots; songs of ascension. But how are we meant to see and celebrate this fullness and blooming when the trees outside are barren?

King David praises God in Psalm 30 with an allusion to the month of Shevat "ארוממך ה' כי דליתני ולא שמחת איבי לי," or "I will exalt you Hashem for you have drawn me up and not let my enemies rejoice over me." The root of the word "דליתני" "to draw" can be understood to come from the word "דלי" meaning bucket, which is the astrological sign for the month of Shevat.

The mystics interpret the same word, "דלי" as relating to "דלת" door.

The Talmud tells us that David's transgression, lusting for a married woman and sending her husband to die in war, wasn't motivated by sin, but it was intended "להורות תשובה ליחיד" to instruct the penitent return of the individual. We are told that the doors to the temple that Solomon built wouldn't open until the merit of King David was invoked. At that moment, the Talmud narrates, the faces of the haters of King David burned like the charred bottom of a pot realizing the one that they labeled as "other" was really the part that they were missing.

It remains clear today, that communal passage into the holiest space is provided by the inclusion of the individual. When we deny entrance to a person who we think has sinned against God, we are all denied access to the Divine. Therefore, King David figuratively becomes a portal that others are welcome to enter through as individuals to come closer to God, demonstrated by the literal doors of the Holy Temple waiting for him to be invited.

Tradition teaches us that the 15th of Shevat is also the day that the sap returns to the tree. Like the soul to the body, the sap provides life and rejuvenation. We elevate ourselves by deepening our sensitivity to see that true life and holiness are often concealed in the protective disguise of feigned insignificance.

Real rebirth and true living come when we emulate the tree that draws from within, in contrast to its perceived, outside value. Tu B'Shevat instructs us to return to the well of spiritual hydration as an individual, for all individuals. While the tree may be barren today, I know that its most powerful source of life is not in the past nor in the passerby, but deep within its roots, that are expanding to provide for the next season of creative growth.

PURIM

BACK TO THE GARDEN: PURIM, PATRIARCHY, AND A PATH FORWARD [26]

The patriarchy begins in response to human beings' primal sin. Eve is told that because she ate (and fed her husband) from the Tree of Knowledge, he will now rule over her (Genesis 3:16). Presumably prior to the sin, Eve and Adam were equal partners, each of them an *ezer k'negdo*, a helpful counterpoint to each other.

In Bavli Eruvin 54a, Rav Acha bar Yakov suggests that the word, חרות or engraved, which is used to describe the Tablets of the Law in Exodus 32:16 can also be read as חרות, meaning freedom. Rabbi Avraham Schorr, in his work *Halekach v'Halebuv* (*Parshat Shekalim*), takes this idea further and suggests that when Israel accepted the Torah at Sinai, they became free from the pall of humans' original sin and they were restored to an Edenic state. Death was vanquished and God's immediate presence could once again be felt by humans. When shortly afterwards Israel commits the sin of the golden calf, they are again catapulted back into a world of transgression, impurity, and gender inequality.

Purim is identified by the Rabbis of the Talmud as a second Sinai. On Purim, the Jewish people accepted the Torah and God's covenant anew (Shabbat 88a). If the original Sinai restored Israel to an Eden-like state, Purim as a Sinai redux should also hold hints of the original spiritual

---

[26] Originally published on March 13, 209 by the Jewish Orthodox Feminist Alliance Blog, co-authored with Rabba Wendy Amsellem

Eden experience.

At first the story of the Purim seems, if anything, to be the opposite of spiritual. The Book of Esther begins with a party that is all about indulgence and excess. There are descriptions of lavish furnishings, abundant wine, and a culture of כי כן יסד המלך לעשות כרצון איש ואיש. Every man's desires were to be fulfilled, at the order of the king. After 187 days of hedony, the party abruptly grinds to a halt when Vashti says no.

In a patriarchal system where the men in power assume their right of access to everything, Vashti's refusal to obey the king is unthinkable. She must be removed immediately, as Memuchan advises, and missives affirming mens' complete domination over women must be at once distributed throughout the empire. A short while later, another person in the Megillah dares to say no. This time it is a man, Mordechai, who refuses to bow to Haman. As Haman himself admits to his entourage (Esther 5:11-13), he has riches and power and status beyond anyone's dreams. Yet, none of it matters to Haman as long as Mordechai refuses to acquiesce to his domination.

The Rabbis of the Talmud connect Haman with the sin of the Tree of Knowledge (Bavli Chullin 139b). Adam and Eve had access to all trees except the Tree of Knowledge. Haman had power over all of King Achashverosh's subjects, except Mordechai. The inability to accept any limits unites the two stories. It is against the backdrop of this unrelenting push to power that Esther finds her voice.

When we are first introduced to Esther in Chapter 2, she is docile and obedient. She goes where she is taken (Esther 2:8, 16); she obeys her guardian Mordechai's every command (Esther 2:10, 20); she asks for nothing of her own, only accepting whatever is given to her (Esther 2:15). She is the ideal woman of the patriarchy, a blank canvas onto whom powerful men can project their desires (Bavli Megillah 13a).

In chapter 4, Esther realizes that it is up to her to save her people. She springs into action, rejecting Mordechai's naive assumption that pleading with the king could be effective if Haman is still in his sphere of influence. Esther orchestrates a master plan, stoking Haman's arrogance and the king's jealousy until she has brought about a fundamental shift in power. She commands Mordechai (4:17) and this time it is he who obeys her instructions.

Esther does not dismantle the patriarchy. At the end of the book, the king is still sovereign and Mordechai is his second-in-command. Esther does get to write her own story, a relatively rare occurrence in the Hebrew Bible. She uses her savvy political awareness to undermine her enemies and save the Jewish people from annihilation. Esther's power suggests a movement back towards a prelapsarian state in which men and women coexist equally and God interacts with humans freely and in a state of grace.

Throughout the Jewish calendar we are invited to focus on specific aspects of daily living which can elevate our spiritual practice. In the Rama's gloss on *Shulchan Aruch, Orach Chaim* 696:8, he explains that celebrating Purim often involved gender bending. Men wore women's clothing and women donned male garb. By dressing up in this manner we are encouraged to think more flexibly about the interplay of gender and power in our lives. For a day we imagine being other then we are, and this allows us to envision the possibility of a differently ordered society.

On Purim, we strive to attain the spiritual clarity of עד ללא ידע, literally "until we don't know," when we no longer limit the spectrum of preoccupation to the rise and fall of male leadership. We encourage everyone to experience Purim as an exercise of expanded equality in Jewish life. Via a temporary return to Eden, we can create a more equitable model for the rest of the year.

I AM A BOY AND THESE ARE MY CLOTHES[27]

"Why are you wearing boy clothes?" This was a question posed by the principal of the Brandeis School, a community day school in New York, to a seven year old transgender student. "These aren't boy clothes! I am a boy, and these are my clothes," the child answered, confused as to how the principal could think that clothing has a gender. The boy's statement was pure and simple, but not enough to stop the school from expelling him for violating the dress code—according to which he conformed as a boy, just not a boy of trans experience.

Gender identity and sexual identity are different, independent, and critical to distinguish in conversations about Jewish law and tradition. For those who choose to shut down conversations about these issues by quoting Scripture, Deuteronomy 22:5 is to gender expression what Leviticus 18:22 is to homosexuality. The verse states: "A man's garment shall not be on a woman, nor shall a man wear a woman's garment, for anyone who does so is an abomination of Hashem." But as I understand it, this verse is the very source that not only permits transgender Jews to wear clothing that supports their gender identity, but also arguably obligates them in doing so.

To understand this reading, let's begin by looking at the issue of cross-dressing on Purim. Purim is a story about the shift from living with a hidden identity to coming out as truly oneself. It is not coincidental that we

---

[27] Originally published on February 28, 2018 by the Jewish Feminist Orthodox Alliance Blog

find expression of this theme in the laws about the holiday. The Rama on *The Code of Jewish Law*, (R' Moshe Isserles 1520-1572) explains:

> There is a custom to wear masks on Purim, for men to wear women's clothing, and for women to wear men's clothing. It is not prohibited because the only intention is to experience happiness and so too [it is not forbidden] to wear garments that contain rabbinically forbidden mixtures.

This passage seems to be revealing a caveat in the scriptural prohibition against cross-dressing. How can something that the Torah forbids, like cross-dressing, become permissible on account of the happiness it brings? Why doesn't Rav Moshe Isserles permit the wearing of biblically forbidden (and not simply rabbinically forbidden) mixtures of wool and linen under the same circumstance? What are we to learn from the comparison of wearing misgendered clothing—ostensibly a biblical prohibition—with "rabbinicialy forbidden mixtures"?

When the Talmud asks where in the Torah we find an allusion to Haman, the evil villain from the Purim story, it brings a verse from the Garden of Eden after the snake causes Adam and Eve to eat the forbidden fruit: "Who told you that you are naked? Have you eaten of the tree from which I commanded you not to eat?" In Hebrew, "from the tree" is *hamin ha-eitz*, which sounds similar to Haman who was also hung on a tree (an *eitz*).

The mystics explain that one of the consequences of eating from that tree was that we lost the letter "aleph" from the word "emet" (aleph-mem-tav), meaning truth, and we were punished with "met," death. The aleph, represents the One, Ruler of the World, whose name is Truth and who can't coexist with perversions of truth. God originally clothed us with light, but after the sin it was replaced with skin, as the garment for the soul. The difference in the Hebrew spelling of light and skin is one letter – "aleph." The fall from light, which is spelled with an "aleph," to skin, which is spelled with an "ayin," expresses the subversive nature of coverings – in this case skin.

Clothing, which we use to cover our bodies, serves as a perpetual reminder of this sin. It reminds us that our spiritual identity is no longer our dominant mode of expression.

We can now reconsider what Scripture meant in Deuteronomy 22:5, when it prohibits cross-dressing. The medieval commentator Rashi explains that the "abomination" is only when a person BOTH presents falsely as another gender, AND with licentious intentions to make it easier to sin by misrepresenting themselves as someone else. It is not, however, referring to someone who wears clothing to give voice to their true gender identity.

It is with this understanding that *The Code of Jewish Law* operates. The rabbis intentionally do not uphold the prohibition against cross-dressing in moments where they might cause pain, where they would be obstacles in the performing of a mitzvah, or in circumstances deemed "uncommon." whose uniqueness needed no specific declaration.

"When we enter into the month of Adar, we increase our happiness." The rabbis interpret this talmudic teaching to allude to the reunification of our intimate coexistence with God. By creating spaces for people to be one with God as their most authentic, genuine, and honest selves, we are restoring the relationship with God in a way that reveals the truth that was lost with the original sin.

Our rabbis teach that on Purim we accepted the Torah again, but this time it wasn't out of fear, like at Mt. Sinai when the mountain was held over our heads. It was out of a unity of love, for God and each other, that brought a new level of acceptance for the differences we have as people, revealing unique aspects of God.

Each year on Purim, we are invited to wear costumes

in order to diminish the role that clothing has in defining us with physical labels. We amplify the voice of our soul that provides awareness of our true identity. By rejecting the right of transgender Jews to wear clothing that most supports their gender identity in religious spaces, it is not only a communal failure of our responsibility to provide sanctuary for all of God's children, but also a denial of the truth of the Torah itself.

ALLYSHIP

NOAH'S ARK: A FAILED ALLY-SHIP[28]

"Justice can never be about just us." Noah, therefore, certainly wasn't a just person – and in many ways, failed at being just a person. For 120 years Noah toiled to build an ark of self-preservation, but didn't invest at all in building a better society. He saved himself, his family, and some animals, but didn't offer a single prayer for the people of his generation. The seminal work of Kabbalah, the Zohar, writes that because of this, God names it the "Flood of Noah" and sees Noah as if he caused the destruction of the world.

At the beginning of the story (Genesis 6:9) Noah is introduced as "a righteous man, perfect in his generations; Noah walked with God." Before the flood (Gen. 7:1) he is no longer perfect, but is still called righteous. After the flood (Gen. 7:23) he survives only as Noah, and then defiles even that basic human identity (Gen. 9:20). He finds himself alive, but not so different from those whom he let die.

He wasn't able to see the Godliness in humanity. Not in others, and in the end, not even in himself. With all the effort towards self-preservation, he failed to preserve even his self.

Rashi interprets "Noah walked *with* God" as "Noah needed support to bear him up." God was Noah's ally and expected him to reciprocate towards God's creations. Rashi contrasts this with Abraham about whom it is written that he (Genesis 17:1) "walk[ed] *before* [God]." He writes: "but Abraham would strengthen himself and walk

---

[28] Originally published on October 7, 2018 by the Bayit Builder's Blog

in his righteousness on his own."

These verses are referenced by the Vilna Gaon (18th century Lithuania) in his commentary on the first entry of the Code of Jewish Law. The Rema, quoting the Psalmist, opens "I have set the Lord before me constantly" (Psalm 16:8); he then adds "this is a major principle in the Torah and among the virtues of the righteous who walk *before* God." The Gaon ends his comments with "and this is the entirety of the virtues of the righteous!"

The difference between one righteous individual and another is simply the degree by which one sees God in the world around them. In the mundane. In nature. In each other.

Abraham saw it; all of our great ancestors did. They prayed, argued, and negotiated with God to save and protect people. When we see something that isn't ok we are meant to do something about it. Faith is a call to action and gives us hope that we can be part of the solution.

This November, there will be an anti-trans referendum on the ballot in Massachusetts that would legalize discrimination against trans folks. Some of us may find ourselves comforted with thoughts of how it doesn't affect us directly – because we don't live there, or because we are cis-gender, or because we don't feel like we need those protections. But this kind of thinking makes us no better than Noah and part of the problem.

Judaism holds us responsible for inaction. It is therefore incumbent upon us, as Jews, to take action – to build a better society, to push back against measures that will hurt the people of our generation, and (if we live in Massachusetts) to vote yes on this referendum for the dignity and respect of all people.

We live in really hard times, with no shortage of things to be outraged about, but God forbid it should ever get easier to see the world being destroyed around us. We must pursue justice for all or soon we will be pursued for being just us.

ALLYSHIP AS SPIRITUAL PRACTICE[29]

Recently, nearly 70% of Massachusetts voted YES on ballot initiative 3, protecting the rights of transfolks against discrimination. This tremendous display of support was brought about by the tireless efforts of transfolks, activists, advocates, and allies. Now that this clear action item has been achieved, we must again ask ourselves: now what? How can we continue to strengthen our sense of communal responsibility, advanced through our quest for inclusivity and human dignity? We witnessed what a powerful result was achieved through the spiritual exercise of networking our resources or "allying up." This is a responsibility that Judaism demands as continual practice, independent of the stakes, high or low.

Our Jewish tradition has embedded within it a deep notion of what it means to be an ally, although the language is not commonly known. Judaism's perspective provides a new framework for this ancient concept. The word "ally" comes from the Latin alligare, bind together. In rabbinic Hebrew, the best term is *chaver* / חבר, a word whose most common translation is "friend." How might our understanding of what it means to be an ally evolve if seen through this interpretive lens?

We find in the Talmud that the word "chaver" has additionally expanded meanings: things connected to the earth are called "mechuber l'karka" and an author is a "m'chaber." What is the linguistic connection between

---

[29] Originally published on November 20, 2018 by the Velveteen Rabbi blog

these three forms of the same word? Our rabbis teach that the word "chaver," at its core, means to attach, whether it is to share the burden with another person, to connect two physical objects, or to manifest thoughts to words and paper.

The Mishnah teaches us "*k'neh l'cha chaver*/acquire for yourself a friend." Perhaps we should understand this directive as a charge to attach ourselves to those who could use support from isolation and marginalization. This is for our benefit; we shouldn't live uninvested in the struggle of another.

It's often hard to stand up for what we believe in, especially when the dominant culture acts in opposition. The Hebrew letter "ו", grammatically known as the *vav hachibur*, the "vav" that attaches, literally models standing up, as the most vertical letter in the Hebrew alphabet. It's shape also embodies a hook and is found in the construction of the Tabernacle - the "vavei hamishkan," the hooks that would connect the curtains to the pillars. In Hebrew grammar it serves the same connective purpose, as the conjunction "and."

In the mystical tradition, the Genesis narrative speaks to the creative power of Hebrew letters. The Hebrew alphabet itself is said to be the building material for creation. Exploring applications of the letter "vav" provides enduring modalities for connectivity and allyship illustrated by the function of the vav in scriptural sources. By examining the ways in which the "vav" is used to connect, in Hebrew grammar, the insights of the Torah can provide new outlooks on how best to parallel our own actions in allyship.

The "vav" is an exceedingly versatile letter with over 15 grammatical functions. The applications of allyship also vary in ways which are person and situation specific. For example, Leviticus 19:2 "Be holy for I am holy/ קדשים תהיו כי קדוש אני." It's noteworthy that the "vav" is missing in the first spelling of קדשים, which refers to our human holiness. The most important prerequisite of allyship is to listen first, and recognize that the voice of the ally is distinctly different. We see God modeling this in God's desire and expectation for us to be fundamentally holy because God, in whose image we are made, is holy. However, we cannot possibly be expected to be the infinite source of the universe. God's request of us is that we should be holy like God, but not wholly like God.

The role of an ally is also different in that it is predicated on the needs of another. We see this beautifully expressed in Esther 4:16, "I with my handmaids." The letter "vav" as a preposition "with" highlights the need to check in *with* those we are trying to support, instead of checking in independently of them, whenever possible.

Additionally, we find an empowering call to universal allyship in Ezra 10:14 "Elders of each and every city." The letter "vav" here means "every" because each and every one of us has the capacity and obligation to be an ally.

However, none of us are meant to be allies all of the time. We can look to Leviticus 21:14 (widow or orphan) where the "vav" means "or." Each of us must be intentional about when, where, and how to step up or away. It is not our obligation to personally fill the void every time and we must be conscious of not taking up too much space.

The "vav" is the sixth letter in the Hebrew alphabet, which alludes to a physical expression of completion: the six days of creation in six directions. It speaks to a world of action being manifested in an embodied way; whether a field being worked, or those doing the work for a six year cycle. There is a unique balance that comes when we invest in toiling for complete equality and liberation; and there is much work still to be done. In Hebrew the "vav" is facing forward, to form a new connection, asking for us "What is the next opportunity to act as an ally, God's ally, in partnering to support all of God's creations?"

ADVANCING THE RABBINIC PRESCRIPTION FOR TRANSGENDER HEALTH CARE[30]

Doctors and rabbis are asked a lot of questions; it's a big part of the job. We certainly don't have all of the answers and so we continue to listen, research, and expand our understanding of different issues. And, we have our own questions to help us get closer to the information that shapes our responses to the people who are asking for guidance. There can be no contradiction between science and religion when they both manifest the truth of the Divine intention. The struggle for that knowledge, and its application, is an ongoing and humbling process.

However, there are still many people in both the medical and Jewish communities who don't yet understand gender identity and transgender experiences. They insist: "It can't be that God put someone in the wrong body. God doesn't make mistakes. It's sacrilegious to change the body that God gave you," and so on. No one would say this about a heart defect, deviated septum, or inflamed appendix – in part because the Torah teaches us in this week's portion: "ורפא ירפא" "and be healed." The Talmud explains that this is the scriptural permission given to physicians offering treatment to change something that God has created.

Similarly, the wicked Turnus Rufus asked of Rabbi Akiva: If your God is a lover of the poor, why then does

---

[30] Originally published on January 31, 2019 by the Hadassah-Brandeis Institute Blog, co-authored with Joshua D. Safer, MD, FACP

God not provide for them? Rabbi Akiva argues that the inequality experienced by many in this world doesn't exist for us to sustain, but rather for us to change. God presents inequality as an opportunity for us to be in partnership, to heal the divide and emulate the Divine by supporting others.

Turnus Rufus replies that by changing the differential that God constructed, we are going against the Divine will and angering God. In response, Rabbi Akiva shares an interesting parable: To what is this similar? It is analogous to a king who, angry with his child, confines them to prison and orders that no one give them anything to eat or drink. Someone then disobeys and provides for the child's needs and when the king hears about it, the king sends the person gifts in thankful recognition. Rabbi Akiva continues: We are all that child to God. When we improve the lives of those who are suffering, it brings pleasure and joy to God.

God, as our parent, wants us to support each other and make sure that we are all provided for.

We demonstrate to God that we see ourselves as God's children when we take care of humanity as we would our immediate family. As a society, we have a responsibility to meet the needs of all, including our transgender siblings. We must make resources available, including all of the resources of modern medicine, whenever needed. It is not only permitted to provide transgender medical procedures, but we are obligated to do so when necessary.

The author of the Shulchan Aruch puts an additional responsibility on doctors to be available to help those in need of their services. He writes (Beit Yosef Yoreh Deah 336): Any doctor who is competent in practicing medicine is obligated to heal and if they hold themselves back from providing treatment, it is considered as if they are a murderer.

Physicians are obligated to learn the optimal

treatments for their patients and to continually extend their knowledge in the hope of ever greater good. Indeed, the scientific mission of the medical community is to develop an increasing appreciation of the complexity of life over time which can then result in better care of fellow human beings.

For many decades, physicians erroneously believed that transgender people suffered from a mental health disorder which required a mental health treatment. Over the past decade or so, the medical community has grown to recognize that gender identity contains a substantial biological component which cannot be altered. There are simply some individuals for whom one part of their biology – their gender identity – is not aligned with another part of their biology – their physical anatomy.

Although the specific biology of gender identity remains an unknown, the current medical approach that is most successful and the standard of good medical care for transgender individuals is to customize treatment to align their physical bodies with their gender identities. Failure to appropriately treat a transgender individual who seeks medical help would be a violation of a physician's professional oath.

Jewish law expects that rabbis rely on the medical opinions of doctors in order to accurately render a response to medical questions. The commentaries are also sensitive to concerns that some Jewish patients might have regarding constantly evolving and new perspectives in the medical profession. The rabbis teach "Don't say that since medicine is just a vocation one shouldn't listen to medical advice because perhaps it will only make the situation worse. It is in response to this that the Torah permits and mandates us to follow the guidance of doctors. One who is punctilious with this is praiseworthy" (Aruch HaShulchan 336:1).

We, rabbis and doctors, must continue to ask questions so that we may better answer the questions we are asked. Some may find it challenging and unfamiliar to respond to new understandings about gender identity, transgender experiences, and treatments. But, it is our obligation, as the field of transgender medicine progresses, to also advance the rabbinic prescription for quality transgender health care.

SHABBOS SHOWS US HOW TO "CHAVER UP"[31]

If you have have wondered how to show up for transfolks, how to be an ally, or "chaver up," the good news is that Shabbos offers us important lessons and insights. Consider it a blueprint for allyship.

On Friday evening, we greet the Shabbos Bride as She presents Herself to us, regardless of our own sexual orientation or gender identity. We don't question Her identity and it doesn't challenge our own. On Saturday we escort Her as a Queen, because that is who She is.

Look also at the language of the special Shabbos additions to the *amidah* which incorporate a gendered arc from the female, to male, and then to the plural pronoun. Friday night the liturgy reads "And in her Israel will rest…" then shifts on Shabbos morning to "And in him Israel will rest…" and concludes Saturday afternoon with "And in them Israel will rest…" Even as God's identity expression transforms from Bride to Queen, from she, to he, to they, we continue to honor God's identity.

Shabbos invites us to meet and experience different aspects of God, in whose image we are all made. It is a weekly invitation to better understand not only God and ourselves, but also ourselves in relationship with God. Although Shabbos, as we know it, is but a 25 hour island of time, its source is in that first Shabbos found in the creation story.

---

[31] Originally published on March 15, 2019 by the Times of Israel Blog, co-authored with Seth M. Marnin

Shabbos is the culmination of all of the physical aspects of creation coming together in unity and purpose. It presents a unique opportunity for us to be present with all of the many parts of ourselves in a heightened awareness of the source of so much of what makes us who we are.

Shabbos supports an exploration above and below the physical limitations of many of our weekday experiences. Although the commandments for the day fit neatly into the binary of positive and negative mitzvot, we are taught that "'To remember and guard' were said in a single utterance, something the [human] mouth cannot speak and something the ear cannot hear." The Rabbis explain that Shabbos is experienced in a supernatural way, with its source in a plane that holds space for things not to be constrained by the physical. We also see this in our ability to accept Shabbos upon ourselves, beginning Shabbos even before the sun has set on Friday evening, and extending Shabbos even after nightfall on Saturday night.

Day and night, male and female, and all in between are held together in one, like the One who created it. The Vilna Gaon, in his commentary to the great love song to God, Song of Songs, explains how Shabbos invites us to be intimate with God in an androgynous way. The word for [God's] "mouth – פיהו," if masculine, should be פיו and if feminine, פיה. By writing it as it does, it presents as both, simultaneously. Additionally, our verse "The sixth day – יום הששי" is understood by the Zohar, as the day of "5 and 6." ה is 5 and ו is six. It is an allusion to the masculine and feminine, the written 5 books of the Bible and the oral 6 Orders of Mishnah, and the positive and negative all coming together on Shabbos in a romantic covenantal partnership of reunification.

At the beginning of the Friday night meal we welcome and introduce ourselves to the angels that visit. This is, perhaps, another exercise to expand our ability to recognize things beyond our own embodied, lived experience.

God has many gendered attributes and names, but no body. When God introduces God's self to Moses, God identifies as "I am who I am." All of the things, all of the time, without tension. The verse that testifies to our Divine image, does so in the plurality of gender, before a split into the binary of Man and Woman. The tradition of gender based spiritual practice supports the idea of gender existing, at least in part, on a soul level. The spectrum of gender that we witness today might be attributed to the fragmentations of souls described in Jewish tradition. Perhaps it is for this reason that we are given an extra soul on Shabbos, to better meet and understand God in gendered ways.

If we take the opportunity to show up for God on Shabbos, if we have the capacity to experience God, whether God is Queen, King, She, He, or They, we are well on our way to appreciating those different from ourselves. By showing up for God, we learn to show up for everyone.

WHAT THE TORAH AND TALMUD TEACH US ABOUT CALLING TRANSGENDER PEOPLE BY THEIR NAMES[32]

Words are powerful. How we use words, how we name things, and what we call people matters. This is especially true for transgender people who change their names. Torah and Talmud have much to teach us about our obligation to respect a transgender person's name change.

Words created the world and still have the ability to change it. The formation of the world began when God said "let there be light." But even before God could say "let there be light," God needed letters to form those words. All the letters of the Hebrew alphabet are therefore the building blocks of creation, בְּרֵאשִׁית בָּרָא אֱלֹהִים אֵת הַשָּׁמַיִם וְאֵת הָאָרֶץ. In the beginning God created "א ת," the first and last letters.

The mystics explain that the life of a person comes from the letters of their name. They reframe the end of Genesis 2:19 נפש חיה הוא שמו (literally, "whatever the man called each living creature, that would be its name") as the life of a living thing is its name.

Names also represent the essence of something. Rashi affirms that the world was created with the "Holy Tongue" because the Hebrew word for "woman," "אשה" *isha*, is related to the word for "man," "איש" *ish* (Genesis 2:23). Man and woman started as one and then were separated.

---

[32] Originally published on June 8, 2018 by *Tablet*, co-authored with Seth M. Marnin.

Their new names, man and woman, reflect that transition in the way new names mirror who we are or who we are becoming.

Just as what we are called reflects who we are, each one of us is a representation of the divine. Our names–the names we are given and the names we claim–influence our purpose in the world. Angels, for example, in Hebrew, are called מלאכים, because they exist exclusively to perform God's work / מלאכה.

But we are not only created in the image of God, we are also messengers of God, each one of us uniquely suited for specific tasks. Sometimes we find that our mission or circumstances evolve and with those new challenges, so too may our name change. When Jacob wrestles with the angel and overcomes the angel, for example, he is told, "Your name shall no longer be Jacob, but Israel…" (Genesis 32:29).

While sometimes name changes follow an event, a new name may be anticipatory or forward looking. The name change might be empowering or assist in the momentum toward the journey. In this week's Torah portion, for instance, Moses gives Hoshea a new name, Joshua, to help him achieve a better outcome when he is sent with the spies to Israel ("Those were the names of the men whom Moses sent to scout the land; but Moses changed the name of Hoshea son of Nun to Joshua") (Numbers 13:16).

How we refer to people, how we respect their names and identities, matters. The Talmud teaches us that it is better to be verbose in order to be sensitive than concise and insensitive. We learn that God added extra letters into the Torah just to show us that it is better to be wordy, and even awkward, if it prevents one from uttering something unrefined (Pesachim 3a).

Recognizing and respecting a name change, one's capacity to change, and the legitimacy of the change is essential, an obligation. In Genesis 17:5, God renames

Abraham, "And you shall no longer be called Abram, but your name shall be Abraham." It is so important to the rabbis that Abraham's new name is recognized and respected they went so far as to argue over whether, if one calls Abraham by his former name, they fail to fulfill the positive mitzvah of calling Abraham by his new name; transgress the underlying prohibition of calling Abraham by his former name implied in the name change; or transgress both at the same time.

R' Zakkai attributed his long life to having, among other reasons, never called someone by something other than their name (Megillah 27b). R' Zakkai was rewarded with long life because he contributed to the life of others by calling them by their appropriate name.

When a transgender person chooses a new name and discards their deadname, it is an act of creation. Like Abraham and Sarah, Israel and Joshua, it is marker. A moment, among moments, of transition and transformation. A new chapter. Renaming ourselves, claiming our names, in order to live our lives is a part of our own holy re-creation. Calling us by our new, correct names is an opportunity for others to contribute to our lives and participate in the holiness.

QUEER ADVICE FROM STRAIGHT RABBIS[33]

Serving the largest LGBTQ synagogue in the world, as two straight rabbis, makes us a little queer. Not because our jobs place us deep in the LGBTQ community, but because here, we are the exception; and being different, in this sense, makes us…queer.

As we prepare for NYC Pride on Sunday, June 24, we wanted to share with you — for those of you who maybe like us are straight, gender conforming, cis rabbis, with the privileges each of these adjectives provides — a few of our thoughts on creating scaffolding that better supports and celebrates, with pride, the opportunities we have to make Jewish communal life both a little more "queer" and a little more "average" for the LGBTQ members of our communities.

When we look at the Jewish calendar, arguably the most festive and outwardly celebratory holiday is Purim. Costumes, masks, parties, and performances frame the festivities. It has been observed that the holiest day of the year — *Yom Hakippurim* / the Day of Atonement — alludes with its name that it is only a day "like" Purim. One interpretation is that it's very easy to feel exceptionally holy on a day that is focused exclusively on spiritual pursuits and individual introspection. But, on a day when we are eating, drinking, and hiding behind our masks in a crowd, it requires more attention to feel truly holy and seen.

---

[33] Originally published on June 15, 2018 as "7 Ways Straight Jews Can Become Better LGBTQ Allies" by the *Forward*, co-authored with Rabbi Yael Rapport

The Purim story of Esther's plight is one of concealed identity and the struggle to publicly acknowledge who she really is. Her name itself means "hidden" and embodies that tension. She was reluctant to reveal her innermost self, until the pain of being quiet outweighed the fear of coming out. She finds herself in circumstances of unparalleled responsibility and opportunity to save the Jewish people — and she delivers. Shockingly, one of the rabbis of the Talmud also interprets her Hebrew name, "Hadassah," as meaning "average."

We find this template of combining both the exceptional and the average in the story of Chana, who is struggling with infertility. When she prays for this most wanted soul, the Talmud (Berachot 31b) recontextualizes her request for "zera enoshim," typically translated as "male offspring," as offspring "inconspicuous among people" — in other words, "average."

Of all the blessings that Chana could wish for her child, why on earth would she choose for them to become average? For those of us who live our lives with our daily choices being comfortably "non-exceptional," we often don't realize what a blessing just being "inconspicuous" can be. In fact, having that level of privilege and the many blessings that come with our definition of "average" is quite exceptional.

The Midrash teaches that in future times, Purim will continue to be celebrated while other holidays will become unnecessary. Perhaps, it will still resonate due to our spiritual evolution — we will embrace a new baseline of radical equality.

So what can we do to better hold space for the unique needs of LGBTQ folks, while also advancing the progress of inclusivity and acceptance?

Listen, and then listen some more.

Allyship is an applied spiritual practice. As people's needs change, so must the resources, and we need to hear it from them.

Know with certainty that in your community, whatever size or description, recognition of LGBTQ experiences matters.

Even if you can name LGBTQ individuals in your communities, it is still likely that someone, who you don't know, is struggling with being closeted, trying to support a family member, and looking to you as a spiritual example for support and understanding.

There can be a large space between inviting folks and making them feel welcomed.

It's very easy to say that services are "open to all," but exceedly difficult to make a synagogue feel like a true sanctuary from the hate, discrimination, and anxiety of the outside world. What are specific, concrete ways your community could hold conversations about specialized needs?

When asking questions about someone's experience or relationship, check internally for the source of your curiosity.

Verbalizing the intention of being helpful and wanting to understand how can go a long way. People are more forgiving of mistakes when they see that the effort to get it right is real.

Normalize speech as an act of progressive inclusivity.

Don't distinguish marriage by the heteronormativity of it; for example calling out "same-sex marriage." There is just marriage. Use person first language in describing anyone from a marginalized segment of society. Invite them to share how they most appreciate being referred to. Please don't minimize it by asking for a "preference." We don't "prefer" that folks use the pronouns that we expect.

Consider positive framing to your language of inclusivity. How does it feel different to say "gender-neutral bathroom" vs "all-gender bathroom?" What about "you are welcome here no matter your gender identity/sexual orientation," vs. "you are welcome here because of who you are," not in spite of it?

Signage - Like the *mezuzah* on a doorpost shows a recognition of Jewish occupancy, Keshet's "Trans Jews Belong Here" initiative acknowledges the space as safe for folk who are trans. Bathroom access is no different. Any gendered space or ritual provides an opportunity to affirm or invalidate the identity of those present and requires a deliberate sensitivity.

Every society is a creation of inclusion and exclusion. Identifying a shared mission and community can help define who we are. In a world that increasingly orients by reaction and rejection of any other identity, let us elevate the most important one — we are all children of the same God. May we, in our regularity, embrace and honor that experience which is exceptional, and in our exceptionality, appreciate our opportunity to elevate the average.

I'M AN ORTHODOX RABBI MARCHING WITH PRIDE[34]

Although the Stonewall raid took place a full decade before I was born, I only heard about June as Pride Month a couple of years ago. It certainly wasn't on the syllabus at my yeshiva. I knew of the Pride Parade, but by a very different name. But this year, for the first time I will be marching in the NYC Pride Parade and taking part in LGBT events throughout the month. Here is why I think you should too.

When God liberated the Hebrews from Egypt they were immediately targeted again, chased by the Egyptians, and finally trapped against the sea. Many were ready to go back to slavery and oppression. One person, Nachshon ben Aminadav, was driven to make sure that advances for freedom and equality were not going to be lost. He walked into the sea, guided by his faith in God's supremacy, and the sea split. It is time for us to walk with faith again. As a country, we have achieved enormous gains in the nearly 50 years since Stonewall, from embracing openly gay people in the military to marriage equality. Today, like at the sea, we are pursuing freedom.

However there is a referendum in Massachuchets this November, that would legalize discriminating against the 1.4 million American trans folks by denying them services in public places like restaurants, hotels, and movie theaters. This administration has tried to ban the 15,000 transgender

---

[34] Originally published on June 1, 2018 by the Jewish Orthodox Feminist Alliance Blog

service people in our armed forces. Adoption and foster care by some married couples is also being threatened around the country.

Do we have enough faith to walk in unity for human dignity and equality, or will we join others who are using faith to elevate themselves through oppressing and enslaving others?

This week's Torah portion, the first of Pride Month, is called Beha'aloscha. Rashi explains that it literally means to "rise up." Tradition teaches that the phrase in this week's *parsha* regarding the "very mighty blow against the people," (Numbers 11:33) was actually a veiled reference to the death of Nachshon. His death came as a punishment for the nation's desire for more privilege and entitlement.

Reb Tzadok of Lublin writes that Nachson's name (נחשון) alludes to the original snake (נחש) *nachash* and the ability to defeat it. Adam and Eve had it really good in the garden, but the snake deceived them to want more. The rabbis of the Talmud saw the true threat of the venomous snake as coming after the bite.

More than the evil inclination wants us to sin, it wants us to feel the toxicity of defeat, after the sin, so that we won't rally to regain our spiritual identity ever again. So too are we most susceptible to hopelessness and paralyzing apathy after we fail to prevent unholy acts of persecution. But we must rally! We can not concede that what we see today is acceptable.

I'm marching because I grew up watching videos of my people being forced on death marches while others were silent and didn't stop it. I'm marching because in my home state of Virginia, Heather Heyer, an American woman, was murdered by a Nazi. I'm marching because the other "pride" rally for the white, straight, you-can-now-leave-your-hoods-at-home type motivates me to refocus my faith in God and rise up, because never again is now!

WANTING TO GET IT RIGHT FOR PRIDE[35]

Growing up in a secular Jewish home in Richmond, Virginia, I was 14 and in Hebrew school when I first encountered Theodor Herzl's teaching, "If you will it, it is not a dream." It blew my mind. What does that mean? There are so many things that I want that aren't realistic. I decided to test it out. I approached a girl I liked and said, "Catherine, I really want to go out with you." Her rejection came without hesitation: "Mike, you're dreaming." So began my complicated journey with Zionism, and women.

I was shocked to find out, years later when I made it to yeshiva, that Herzl's teaching actually has its source in the Rabbinic tradition. The Chida (18th century Jerusalem) wrote "nothing stands in front of a person's will" and the Talmud testifies "whichever way a person wants to go they take him."

The Rabbis point out the difficulty with such a theology; how can this concept obtain when we have the competing truth of: *אונס רחמנא פטריה* -*onus rachmana patrie* (the Torah exempts a person when things are beyond one's control). If I find myself in a forced circumstance that is no fault of my own, why isn't it just an indicator that I didn't want it badly enough?

They share a beautiful insight from the story of creation about God's process of negotiating competing interests that provides a fascinating and comforting outlook at the intersection of LGBT and Israeli complexities. The medieval exegete Rashi writes on the

---

[35] Originally written in June of 2018

opening verse in the Bible: "At first, [God] thought to create [this world] through the strict Attribute of Judgment, but saw that it wouldn't be sustainable, so God gave precedence to the Attribute of Mercy and joined it to the Attribute of Strict Judgment." In other words, God's compassion and mercy are prerequisites for us to coexist with God, because we all struggle and make mistakes.

The Sefas Emes explains that in the world of "thought" - what a person wants - the strict attribute of judgment still obtains. How can we defend wanting to be unhealthy, insensitive, or ungrateful? However, in the world of action, there is no shortage of reasons why we fall short of actualizing the ideal; all you can eat buffets, not getting enough sleep, and life's distractions. So God provides compassion and mercy when we want to get it right, but haven't yet figured out how.

This is what the Chida means that nothing stands in the way of a person's desire; there are no excuses and there is no one to blame - we have visions and aspirations for ourselves and we are solely responsible for them. In that space, Herzl agrees, if we will it, it is not a dream.

It seems that the compassion, forgiveness, and mercy come only once those first givens of good intentions are established. Perhaps a way to narrow the space between folks, who find coexistence with an other that seems dangerous to be a struggle and threatening, is by first recognizing the shared desire of wanting to live in peace while still holding all of our identities and shortcomings.

Tradition teaches in the context of God's vision of creating this world, סוֹף מַעֲשֶׂה בְּמַחֲשָׁבָה תְּחִלָּה - *sof ma'aseh b'machshavah techilah*, what would be enacted in the end, started first as thought. What would become Saturday evening, the beginning of the time of separation - havdalah - was exactly the moment of the Divine thought of creation and the beginning of the unification of all that was destined to exist.

The dream of coming together, as individuals and as

humanity, was the beginning of God's process towards peace and wholeness. How might our process of inclusivity and expansive tolerance be advanced if we refocused on shared goals and hopes?

This month of pride, coming at a time of such violence and divisiveness, compels us to reaffirm that what we see today is not God's will. This is not God's dream - nor is it any of ours. With all of the pain and suffering in Israel, and in America, no one is living the dream.

I was proud that I took a chance with Catherine, and compassionate with myself when it didn't work out. It wasn't the last time I was told to "keep dreaming" and I have followed that wise advice. We need to celebrate, with pride, our desire to get it right by loving compassionately those who think that we have gotten it wrong.

ONE STRAIGHT, WHITE, CISGENDER RABBI'S ROLE AS AN ALLY[36]

I was approached last week, after a speech I delivered on transgender inclusivity, and was asked if I had transitioned from female to male. I felt confusion, discomfort, and kinship with all of those who suffer the humiliating injustice that comes from the socially constructed entitlements of others. I wanted to stand with them in solidarity, all children of one God, and somehow help absorb this blow to human dignity.

My initial thought was to respond "Does it make a difference?" instinctively saying to myself, "All lives matter!" Instead, I replied "No," because it does make a difference.

The voice of an ally isn't the same voice as the one who's been oppressed, marginalized, and struggled against being silenced.

My name is Mike. I'm white, straight, and a cis-gender male. My father is a doctor, as was my grandfather, and I grew up in the suburbs. When I get pulled over by the police, after they see my license, registration, and clergy parking, they often ask for a blessing — and never ask me to step out of the vehicle. I also work full time in social justice and, yeah, sometimes it's awkward, because the systems of oppression that are in place, that we are fighting against, are designed to benefit me, and they have.

I don't need access to more space and to co-occupy

---

[36] Originally published in June of 2017 on the Auburn Theological Seminary Website (auburnseminary.org)

one of vulnerability, especially with preserved asymmetry, can only be offered as an invitation that still requires consent from the one exposed.

I don't feel rejected when I volunteer to spend May Day swiping a MetroCard for those who find it hard to pay the fare to get to work and am told that I'm not welcomed because I'm white.

However, when people who have the resources, power, and agency but choose not to extend, expand, and use those spaces for good, I'm offended on a soul level. I perceive it as a perversion of the Divine truth, the truth that God is everywhere all of the time and that everything belongs to God.

God made space for us, and it is God who asks that we echo that holiness by making space for others.

When we see someone or a group of people who are weakened, exposed, and forced into inhumane postures of fragility, this physical weakness gives amplified expression to the screams of their soul — a soul yearning to be held with a respectful acknowledgment of its divine origin. And if we don't protest this sacrilegious reality, what does our silence reveal about the condition of our soul?

In the Jewish tradition, we offer condolences by invoking a specific aspect of God: הַמָקוֹם יְנַחֵם אֶתְכֶם — *Hamakom yenachem etchem* ("May the Omnipresent comfort you").

Of the many different names for God, we use *Hamakom* ("the Omnipresent," or literally, "the Place"), here as a comforting reminder that no space or circumstance is free from the Divine Presence. By preventing sanctuary, equality, or inclusion, we contribute to the denial of that comfort to humanity.

Spiritual practice demands social consciousness. If a person's physical, emotional, or mental health is harmed through the denial of human rights or other oppression, then the soul is also limited in its expression. We thereby exclude God from God's entitled space and allyship.

If we want God as our mother, father, parent, then we need to see each other as brothers, sisters, siblings. When we get hurt, we scream out. Not because it helps alleviate the pain, but because if we don't scream when we are privileged to, then it doesn't really hurt.

When people are suffering, it is the silence that is awkward.

TRANSITIONING TOWARDS GOD[37]

Borrowing language from the queer community, I was assigned secular at birth, identified as Ultra-Orthodox for about 20 years, and now see myself as some version of religiously nonconforming. At 17 I came out as observant and at 37 as an ally. First privately, as I tried to understand the gender transition of someone in my immediate family, and then very publicly in response to a trans student at Columbia who was really struggling. There is a way in which my path to this moment has been a very linear progression, one natural choice leading to the next. And there is also a way in which at 37 I felt just like I did at 17; trying to understand the Divine will and struggling to answer the exact same question we are all meant to ask ourselves: who am I really?

On my first Shabbos in the fall of '96, I'm in shul Friday night in Richmond, VA, introducing myself to the rabbi and some of the congregants when another rabbi comes over to me and says with a huge smile, "So this is our newest baal teshuva." I smiled back, having no idea what that was, or if it was even a good thing. I'm still not completely sure.

Walking back from shul, I asked my host, "What was that Hebrew phrase?" He explained to me "It means one who has mastered the return." I remember thinking: what a low bar...right, I've been keeping Shabbos for like 2 hours and I'm already an expert.

---

[37] Originally delivered as a drashah on June 8, 2018 at Congregation Beit Simchat Torah

But it's true, our natural habitat is one of spirituality. We, as humanity, must elevate and protect that source, recognizing that the most pronounced identity of any human being is that of being created in the image of the Almighty. It's a difficult journey to get there, for all of us, but when we do arrive, we know that we are at home.

This is the advice that God gives to Abraham, לך לך (lech le'cha) / go towards yourself. Be the most genuine and authentic version of you that you can be. Explore. Evolve inwardly. Reflect to the universe your unique blend of beautiful holy Godliness.

Moses, in the beginning of this week's *parsha* is also told by God שלח לך אנשים (Numbers 13:2) translated as "send forth for yourself men," in the context of searching out the goodness of the land of Israel. I understand it additionally as שלח לך-- אנשים "folks, search yourselves out." Go see how good you really are.

So where do we go to look? How are we meant to see the goodness in the complexity of our identities and imperfections?

The mystics explain that this "land" that we are sent to inherit, is the formative material that God gathered to mold us into who we are. Adam is called אדם because they were made, מן האדמה (*min ha'adamah*) or from the ground. That specific earth, tradition tells us, is found under the altar in Jerusalem. There is holiness in coming together, echoing the Divine through unity. It is deliberately that place, where heaven and earth join, that invites us to make an offering to God.

The Talmud teaches that when partnerships fail and there is separation, it is the same altar that cries.

Our bodies host our souls and the choices we make are the sacrifices we bring to God.

The Arizal, 16th century Safed, teaches that those twelve men that were tasked by Moses with scouting Israel, were incarnations of the twelve sons of Jacob. It is alluded to in Genesis 42 when Joseph says to his brothers

מרגלים אתם / you are spies, who have come to see the land.

There is a beautiful insight from Reb Yerucham of the Mir that provides a helpful outlook on the exploration of individualized contributions. When Jacob gathers his sons to give them each a blessing, everyone gets their own, except for Shimon and Levi. It wasn't just because they get yelled at; Reuven also is rebuked. The scriptural asymmetry and structural abnormality of this deviation invites the reader to ask, "What truth is being concealed here?"

The verse says "Simeon and Levi are brothers, stolen tools are their weapons." Rashi explains that the craft of "living by your sword" belongs to Esav, their uncle, but they deployed it in attacking Shechem. Reb Yerucham observes that when we are present as ourselves, then each and every one of us is deserving of our own custom blessing, but as soon as we pretend to be someone we are not, then we are like all of the other folks denying the world our own personal one of a kind contribution.

We have a holy responsibility, to make all space safe, especially for trans folks. You are a blessing.

The need to be seen and understood doesn't have its source in the human experience, but rather in the Divine. The Midrash frames the original emptiness and void as God's loneliness. Perhaps God made billions of different faces because it gives God a better chance of being seen and understood for who God is.

The Talmud highlights a way in which God differs from us. The greatness of God is that when we mint a coin, each one is the same as the others, but when God made us, each equally in God's image, we are all different. It is specifically in what makes us different from each other that God's greatness is most visible.

God is a giver. It's not good for us to be alone because we are created in the image of God and it's not good for God to be alone. We are also givers. Our most precious gifts to the universe are the embodied contributions that only each one of us in our own uniqueness can make.

Like Hillel taught: "If I am not for myself, who will be for me." because no one else is me. But "if I'm only for myself, what am I?" For who we are, at our essence, also requires a posture of creative production.

This denial of our capacity for expansiveness was the true sin of the spies. The verse says "We were like grasshoppers in our eyes, and so too we were in their eyes" (Numbers 13:33). They adopted the identity of who they thought people saw them as. They were afraid to embrace their true, powerful identities because there are consequences for stepping into the voids of this world that no one else can fill. Often it is lonely.

It takes a lot of courage to speak one's truth to the world. It's not a small thing and it's something to be very proud of.

In the Jewish tradition, being proud of pride takes a lot of humility. When Moses was ready to deploy the scouts to check out the land of Israel, he was nervous that Hoshea, was actually too humble. So he changed his name to Yehoshua.

Now Moses is an expert on humility; after all the Bible wrote about him that he was the humblest of all men on the face of the earth (Numbers 12:3). So why is it perceived as a deficiency in Hoshea? Additionally, how does adding a "י" to "הושע" / Hoshea to make "יהושע" / Yehoshua, help?

The Talmud in Megillah observes that wherever we find mention of God's might, it is immediately followed by God's humility. For example, "For Hashem your God is the God of the heavenly forces, and the Master of masters" (Deuteronomy 10:17) is immediately followed in the next verse with "[God] performs justice for the orphan and widow."

There is a way in which we are more complicated than God. As the infinite source of the universe, God is everywhere, all of the time. We occupy a physical and finite space. On that surface, it is often this to the exclusion of that. But above and below, on the spiritual level, everything can be held without contradiction.

How great is repentance, says the Talmud, that the entire generation is forgiven. It doesn't mean that as long as one of us gets it right, we are all good, that would be too easy. Rabbi Akiva Eiger offers some clarity through a Kabbalistic interpretation that we each, in our own individual souls, also hold the souls of all of the other folks who are alive. So when one person repents, that portion of the soul in everyone in the entire generation is forgiven. It's the same source that allows one person to make kiddush for another. *Kol Yisrael aveivim zeh la'zeh*, all of Israel serve as guarantors for each other. *Aruv* also means mixed up. We are literally all in this together.

In this struggle for dominant expression of competing parts, lies the holiness. In Kabbalat Shabbat we say *Ohr Zarua L'Tzadik* - the light is planted for the righteous *U' l'Yisrael simcha* - the aligned heart is happy. It's hard to feel joy in the struggle. It's all too easy to feel sad in the tension.

A rebbe of mine used to say "It's much easier to fail a test than it is to pass it." The tzadik, righteous person, falls seven times and gets up. It's the throwing ourselves back into the fight after failure that is worthy of praise.

The prophet Habakkuk 2:4 teaches "The righteous live with their faith." Not just that we live our lives and makes choices based on faith, but we have the faith that we can fail seven times and still be called righteous.

The brother of the Maharal of Prague observed that this struggle is represented in the letter Tzadik itself- צ. It is really two letters: the Nun "נ", which stands for falling and which is why it is bent over, represents the body going back to its source, the earth. The other part is the Yud- י. *Pintele yid* - the unique piece from God that is also trying to go back to its source.

On some level it's the most horrible *shidduch* ever.

Ostensibly they want completely different and mutually exclusive things. It also makes the world unpredictable because we don't know what will find strength in the moment.

It was this fear that motivated Moses to add the "י" to Hoshea's name. His new name, Yehoshua ben Nun–Joshua the son of Nun - speaks to this transition. He now leads with the "י." The Jerusalem Talmud says that the "י" also transitioned from the female at the end of Sari's name, before it is changed to Sarah, - being repositioned at the head of the male Joshua.

There are no extra people in this world. God loves us more than we could possibly love ourselves. We are all sent here, as messengers of the Almighty, to push away darkness and to chase joy.

Both Talmuds teach "[A]n emissary of a person is like the person themselves." Homiletically, I think it means that our purpose in being sent here, is to be us. And the constant question, for me at least, is now what?

The Midrash answers "Ein atah elah teshuva." The concept of now, is only about returning to our source. The choices that we have made in the past, that might have distanced us from the Source, does not at all limit or define how close we can come to it in the future. When we find Shalom as wholeness, then it is easier for us to find Shalom as peace. The world needs you and will never be the same without you.

WRESTLING WITH MOURNING ON TRANSGENDER DAY OF REMEMBRANCE[38]

November 20th is Transgender Day of Remembrance (TDOR). It is a day of mourning, a day to remember and honor the lives of those who were lost to anti-transgender violence. We recall both the ones whose names we know and those we don't. Each one a universe. Each one irreplaceable. Each one a unique child of God.

But how can we do justice to their memories and mourn their loss, when we find ourselves inundated with tragedy, sometimes numb to the pain so that we ourselves may survive? How do we honor a day of mourning when every day feels like a day of mourning? We are bombarded with tragedies: the massacre of Jews in Pittsburgh; a mass shooting at a bar; dozens killed in California fires; voter suppression across the country; the senseless murder of people of color. It's hard to recount all of the horrific traumas and tragedies of just the past few weeks, much less of the last year.

Our rabbis teach us that there is a difference in the way we process the mourning and remembrance of a personal loss and that of a historic or communal one. For a collective loss, we start slowly and build, recalling each event and its accompanying sadness and then move into a more intense time of mourning. The Three Weeks is a good example of this. This period of mourning recalls the braking of the two tablets that Moses brought down from

---

[38] Originally published on November 20, 2018 by the Times of Israel Blog, co-authored with Seth M. Marnin

Mount Sinai. It begins on the 17th of Tammuz and leads up to the destruction of the First and Second Temples three weeks later on the 9th of Av. It reflects this slow progression of mourning – where we decrease our joy over a period of time, eliminating foods and activities that bring us pleasure, culminating in the fast of Tisha B'Av.

In contrast, however, when it comes to a loss of someone in our family, God forbid, the order is reversed. The first seven days of *shiva* is the most intense, primary period of mourning. For 30 days, the period of *sheloshim*, there is a secondary, less intense period of mourning when mourners return to most regular activities but continue to observe certain restrictions. And then when mourning the death of a parent, there is an additional 11-month period, *shanah*, where there are the fewest restrictions for the mourner as a way to reintegrate into a world that is now missing a loved one.

This distinction between individual mourning and collective or historic mourning makes sense. When we lose someone close to us, we don't need structure to help us acknowledge the moment, to get us into a space where we can feel its power. To the contrary, when we lose a loved one, we need scaffolding to help us process our overwhelming and often incapacitating feelings in a way that allows us to move forward.

For some, TDOR may feel more like remembering the destruction of the Temple on Tisha B'Av — perhaps because we don't know any of the transgender people who were murdered, or because we may not feel vulnerable in the same way because of our race or class privilege, or because we are cisgender. For others, whether we feel a particular connection to victims of anti-trans violence or not, we are so overwhelmed by daily news of gun violence, the attempted erasure of transgender people by the administration, the surge of white nationalism, and the ravages of climate change, that we are anesthetized to these deaths, unable to meaningfully remember as we are called to do.

Whether we require a slow progression to reach the spiritual and emotional place to mourn those murdered as a result of anti-transgender violence or we experience it as the acute loss of a loved one, remember we must. As Jews, we have a communal responsibility to feel the pain of others and to do something about it. We cannot accept a society where some people are treated as less human than others.

Remembering, not unlike Jacob's wrestling in this week's Torah portion, Miketz, is a call to action. Jacob finds himself alone when he returns for the "small vessels," a metaphor for Jacob leaving his family and returning for those who were left behind (Genesis 32:25). It is in this moment — Jacob remembering those left behind — that his worthiness to lead a nation is revealed, and with it a new name; Israel. Another noteworthy consequence of Jacob's wrestling with the angel is that we, as his descendants, are no longer allowed to eat from the displaced sinew (hindquarters), the *gid hanashe*, which the Zohar says corresponds to the 9th of Av. This prohibition is to remind us that the struggle for equality and inclusivity – not leaving anyone behind – is one that we each must fight for in every generation.

TDOR provides us all with an opportunity. Our rabbis teach that the best way to remove the evil of the world is by doing good. In remembering and honoring the memories of the transgender people lost this year to bigotry and violence – that is, leaving no one behind — we recommit to transform the world by ending transphobia. Whether in our words or deeds, through legislation, in religious communities, or elsewhere in the world, on this Transgender Day of Remembrance, let us wrestle with everything we have to end the fear, hatred, and violence.

WORLD AIDS DAY AND THE ROLE OF THE RIGHTEOUS[39]

This week's Torah portion starts with: וישב יעקב בארץ מגורי אביו בארץ כנען.

"Now Jacob was settled in the land where his father had sojourned, the land of Canaan" (Genesis 37:1).

Rashi explains:

וישב AND IT WAS SETTLED — Jacob wished to live at ease, but trouble with Joseph suddenly came upon him. When the righteous wish to live at ease, the Holy One says to them: "Are not the righteous satisfied with what is stored up for them in the world to come that they wish to live at ease in this world too!" (Genesis Rabbah 84:3)

It is our desire to detach from the struggle, that itself generates it. Jacob felt like he had made it and just wanted to take a break. It is consequently at that moment that Joseph is sold. It feels like we are at a similar place around AIDS. As there have been significant medical advances in recent years, a narrative of progress has developed in the mainstream, and as the perceived urgency is diminished, marginalized communities locally and internationally remain affected. It is our underlying complacency that got us to this place; we haven't really fixed the problem at all. It is time to raise up the struggle for equality as the role of the righteous.

"And I think that for me it's never been just about

---

[39] Originally published on November 30, 2018 on the Talk To Me About HIV website (talktomeabouthiv.org), co-authored with Jesse Katz

fighting the AIDS epidemic. To me it's always been about the drivers that have been behind the AIDS epidemic because I'm quite sure that in my lifetime not only will we end AIDS as an epidemic but we will also find a cure. But if we don't at the same time find a cure for racism, for homophobia, for transphobia, for stigma that's put on people who use drugs, if we don't find cures to address those things, the fact of the matter is there's always another virus out there lurking to take advantage of our inhumanity." – Charles King, CEO of Housing Works

One of the deepest lessons the AIDS epidemic teaches, and the importance of learning its history, is that the devastation is not just a result of the virus itself, but the ways in which communities are marginalized. The virus had allies in every individual who refused to recognize the inhumanity of their ambivalence, or inaction. History also demonstrates that it is always the communities who are most vulnerable that are hit hardest, communities that are not protected by the privilege of the majority. Mainstream reaction is slow, uncommitted, and often unproductive when catastrophe hits our marginalized communities. In these moments, we see the detriment of our passivity. To not reach out and help, is to deny one's own humanity.

With the onset of the digital age, we are inundated with information that can leave us numb and despondent. It is so important to not despair, and remain engaged. As we make our mental calculations about what we actually have the emotional bandwidth for, it is important to remember that love has no maximum capacity, that you can never run out of 'thank you's,' 'I'm sorry's,' or 'I love you's.' There is a false notion that less love, less engagement, less opening up of yourself to vulnerability will somehow protect you, when in actuality that exposure is what allows you to be blessed and to heal.

This World AIDS Day we remember those we have lost, and in doing so we also remind ourselves of the holiness and radical strength of love. We are more ourselves when we connect with each other and ultimately we draw strength from each other, opening ourselves up for healing together.

IN DARK TIMES, BE A LIGHT[40]

On Chanukah we celebrate the miracle of light — which can feel challenging when we are surrounded by so much darkness, both physically through short winter days and spiritually by the increase of hate and oppression around the world. It's especially challenging because the light that we each bring is so often separated from one another. Our souls are isolated, so our lights are too. Chanukah teaches us how to overcome that separation by adding light to light.

We each have our own list of the various sources of darkness in our lives, and there are many. Hate crimes are on the rise, bigotry and racism have become increasingly emboldened, we face the daily grind of struggling against more and more oppressive policies at every turn. How can we be real about the darkness without being Pollyanna or pretending it doesn't hurt people, while at the same time cultivating the inner resources we need to bring light?

Perhaps the real miracle of Chanukah is learning to see, even in darkness, our obligation to banish that darkness with light. After all, that's how God answered the original darkness — *va'y'hi ohr*, "let there be light." Made in God's image, we too have the capacity to bring light.

We have an opportunity to further develop this ability during Chanukah — and also each week as Shabbos comes to its close. At havdalah we banish darkness with the unifying light of a multi-wicked candle, representing our

---

[40] Originally published on December 5, 2018 by eJewish Philanthropy, co-authored with Rabbi Rachel Barenblat and Victoria Cook

souls coming together to create change, transitioning from the restorative sweetness of Shabbos as we act toward building a better world.

Saturday night we return to a position of creative work, in partnership with God, after making the blessings of havdalah. #BeALight, a joint project of Bayit: Your Jewish Home, Congregation Beit Simchat Torah, and Torah Trumps Hate, invites just that. Each week at havdalah we publicly commit on social media to a concrete step toward building a world of greater justice (for example, "this week I will attend a protest for..." or "this week I will volunteer my time for..." or "This week I will speak out against injustice X," or "This week I will give tzedakah to Y.") And then we invite friends to join us in building that world of justice, human dignity, and hope.

For those who already have a practice of making havdalah, #BeALight is an invitation to begin the new week with a concrete action toward building a better world, coming together like the flames of the multi-wicked candle. For those who already have a practice of engaging in social justice work, #BeALight is an oppertunity to sanctify that work by rooting it in havdalah.

And as for our weekly havdalah, so too for our nightly kindling of Chanukah candles. Each one is an opportunity to rededicate ourselves to building a world of renewed justice and love.

Our spiritual ancestors took action to purify the Beit HaMikdash. Now at Chanukah we follow in their footsteps, purifying our hearts through engaging in acts that bring light to the world.

The Shelah writes that the 36 candles we light over the course of Chanukah correspond to the 36 hours we communed with God in the Garden of Eden. Each night when the Chanukah candles gleam, we remember the hidden light of creation – just as, during havdalah when we hold our hands up to the braided candle, we can glimpse our hidden nature as beings of light, and remind ourselves of the time in the garden that came before the pain of separation.

Our tradition teaches that part of the original light of creation was reserved for the righteous. The light of each Chanukah candle is also designated as holy – it's holy and can not be used for anything mundane. Its purpose is just to be. Simply by existing, the Chanukah lights remind us of the miracles that sustained us in days of old and continue to reverberate in our day. When we look upon those lights this year, how will we be inspired to #BeALight in the world around us?

Just as the menorah in the window tells the world that we celebrate the miracle of the few successfully fighting for the rights and dignity for all, so too we advance the cause when we post, update, or tweet about our commitment to #BeALight, sharing our light with the world.

In a havdalah candle, flames come together to create something greater than the sum of their parts. As we light the chanukiyah, each night there is more light than the night before. When we choose to #BeALight and urge others to join us, we too can create more light than before.

The Chanukah candles can represent the strength and sacrifices of all of those brave souls who came before us, risking everything so that we could live and love and be whole. When you light the chanukiyah this year, when you light your havdalah candle each week, what light will you bring into the world? What do you want your candle to be?

HOW GOODLY ARE YOUR RAINBOW TENTS[41]

This week, we read *Parshat Balak* in the Book of Numbers. The portion begins as the Israelites, wandering through the desert, approach the nation of Moab. Balak, king of Moab, asks Balaam, a non-Israelite diviner, to curse the Israelites out of fear of what the Israelites might do to his people. After much back and forth, Balaam agrees to go, on the condition he speaks only what God speaks. To Balak's disappointment, Balaam follows God and blesses the Israelites in the end: *Ma tovu ohalecha*, How goodly are your tents, O, Jacob, Your dwellings, O Israel! (Numbers 24:5).

We see Balaam's words, originally a curse, turn into a blessing. It was with that same sense of openness to different positions and perspectives that we, the co-authors of this piece, came to sit together. We met for the first time at the Religious Action Center of Reform Judaism in Washington, D.C. Like Balaam and the Israelites, we, too, are an unlikely pair to find a blessing. We are a rabbi with three ultra-Orthodox ordinations – whose transgender relative's coming out set his life on a path of trans activism – and a young professional working for the Reform Jewish Movement who discovered her passion for trans issues through anger at the rescinding of Title IX protections for students in public schools.

As we spoke, we asked questions, not with accusation

---

[41] Originally published on June 25, 2018 on the Reform Judaism website (reformjudaism.org), co-authored with Lizzie Stein

but with curiosity. We listened to each other, not with skepticism but with openness. An uncomfortable and hesitant meeting turned into a cacophonous brainstorm of ideas for partnership, driven by a simple shared goal: justice and rights for all LGBTQ people inside and outside the Jewish community, especially transgender and gender non-conforming folks.

In the phrase "Ma tovu ohalecha," transition from solo spiritual practice to communal responsibility is reflected as the verse shifts from the temporary holiness in the tents of Jacob as an individual to the permanent dwellings of the collective Israel. Jewish tradition teaches that Jacob earned this blessing by fighting for the most vulnerable and marginalized of our people. Today, we follow in that tradition by fighting for transgender equality.

To act on this communal responsibility and bring our Jewish values into the public square, to see as blessings those who have been falsely cast as curses, the Reform Movement is embarking on a new, nonpartisan campaign, Civic Engagement: Every Congregation Counts, Every Vote Counts. This campaign aims to empower Reform Jews to act collectively to exercise their right to vote and ensure that Jewish voices and values are present this election season.

It is fitting that the campaign begins during Pride Month. We must be visible in our support of the LGBTQ community, and one way to do that is to make our values visible by voicing them publicly and staying active in our communities.

This November, transgender rights are on the ballot in Massachusetts. In 2016, a bipartisan majority of the Massachusetts General Court (state legislature) passed SB 2407, which prohibits discrimination on the basis of gender identity in public accommodations. Opponents of this legislation have gathered enough signatures to put a veto referendum on the ballot. A "yes" vote will uphold SB 2407 and protections for transgender people in

Massachusetts. We must organize to ensure the rights of transgender and gender diverse people in Massachusetts – turning curses into blessings and bringing our values to the forefront from now until November.

The Talmud teaches that the Second Temple, described as God's dwelling place on earth, was destroyed because of unnecessary hatred. By showing love instead of hatred to all God's children, especially those who have been denied access and equality in our tents, we are worthy of Divine blessings for peace and goodness. We, as the Jewish people, must work harder to be more visibly united with each other so our tents, too, may be good.

THE TORAH OF ACTION[42]

The Torah was given on the low mountaintop of Sinai to equate that vantage point, which offered the best view to navigate the surrounding valley, with the insights of the Torah, which provide an outlook on how to best walk through life. A commitment to action was a prerequisite to receiving the Torah. We said, "We will do and we will listen!" When we hear of social injustices, like the bill in Massachusetts that would make it legal to deny services to trans people in movie theaters, restaurants, hotels, and other public spaces, the Torah instructs us to take action to preserve both human dignity and our values.

Keshet is leading the Jewish mobilization effort as part of a statewide coalition, Freedom for All Massachusetts. The campaign will kick off with a Jewish Community Town Hall to Defend Trans Equality in partnership with Freedom for All Massachusetts and Hebrew College on Monday, May 14 and will continue up through Election Day.

The evening of May 14th is also Rosh Chodesh Sivan, the beginning of the month when the Torah was given. In the mystical tradition, Sefer Yetzirah teaches that this month is governed by the letter "ז" *zayin*, which corresponds to motion (הליכה) and to the tribe of Zebulon. The Torah was intentionally given during the month relating to the tribe that was known for going out into the world (Deuteronomy 33:18), because it is meant to be applied in the world through a theology of practice. It is

---

[42]Originally published on May 11, 2018 by the Keshet Blog

not enough to love peace, we must also pursue it.

The Zohar explains that the letter "ז", which literally means armaments, speaks to how we are meant to fight against oppression and discrimination through our communal strength in support of righteousness. Halacha, Jewish law, means to walk or go, *holech*, because it obligates us to show up in the streets for what is true and just. The Talmud teaches that after the destruction of the temple, the only place where God is found in this world is in the four cubits of Halacha. It is in the forward motion of advancing radical inclusion, perfected at Mt. Sinai when we were like one person with one heart, where God is found.

This week's Torah portion starts with the Divine promise that "if we go out" (תלכו) with the Torah, then God will provide for us to dwell securely. In response to this offensive bill we are required to "go out" and partner with the Almighty to make sure that all of God's children can dwell securely. If we don't fight against the erasure of truth and equality, then we surrender to a society of fake holiness.

The light of the Torah is here to dispel the darkness of this world. Please join me at the town hall meeting and mobilize to defeat this unjust bill.

IT'S A BIG TORAH[43]

I'm writing this as the family member of a transgender child, who feels constricted in a space too narrow to accept them, as well as so many of God's other children, as equals. I'm also frustrated, as someone who identifies as some version of traditional, at how small we have made the Torah and the limits that we have put on God and holiness. It is my belief that by expanding the tent of Torah, we can get closer to understanding how big and inclusive it really is.

It isn't good for humans to be alone because we are created in the divine image and it isn't good for God to be alone. Was the void that God felt in the beginning when there was no one to see or try to understand God, so different from our feelings of loneliness or our need to be held and understood? Our struggle to find a place to belong and be loved for who we are isn't just a part of the human experience, but rather it echoes the Divine.

The Book of Genesis opens with a large Hebrew letter "bet" (ב), beginning the first word of the Torah, "בראשית" (Genesis). The letter "bet" is formed by connecting a vertical line with two horizontal lines. These three lines represent a unifying act of construction. Two parallel lines can be extended forever, but they will always need a third line to bring them together: finding commonality among differences is the framework of every

---

[43] Originally published on November 7, 2016 as "Reflections from an Orthodox Rabbi with a Trans Child" by the Keshet Blog, under the pen name Kol Raychaim

partnership, including God's relationship with us. When we spell out the letter "bet" in Hebrew we get the word "בית," ("bayit") meaning house. Perhaps the Torah starts with this letter to teach us that we are all guests in God's house.

There is another unifying aspect of the letter "bet" in "בראשית", as a prefix to the rest of the Torah's first word "ראשית," meaning beginning or first. Usually only one thing can be considered first in any category, but our tradition teaches that there are actually three firsts; God, Torah, and the Jewish people. The Zohar writes that all three are connected and in truth, all three are the same. The "bet" alludes to this concept when we see it as the letter and simultaneously, as three lines or three of the letter "ו" "vav"s that form the "ב."

In Hebrew, the word for the conjunction "and" exists only as the prefix "ו," which is also the letter "vav." Its job is to connect one thing and another. The "vav" gets it name from the "וו, vavei, the hooks in the tabernacle that connected the curtains to the pillars. Indeed, the letter, when written properly, looks like a hook. There are three different ways that we find the letter "vav" spelled out: "ואו," "ויו," and "וו" with corresponding numerical values of 13, 22, and 12. These allude to the oneness of the Creator, (אחד – one, whose Hebrew letters add up to 13 in numerology), the twenty two letters of the Hebrew alphabet in which the Torah was written, and the twelve tribes of Israel. God, Torah, and the Jewish people coming together as one supportive structure.

It is perhaps not coincidental that when Cain finds himself an exiled wanderer feeling afraid, vulnerable, and exposed, the sign that God places on his forehead is the connecting letter "vav" "ו." The Hebrew word for life or soul, *neshamah* "נשמה," is the same as the word for barren or desolate. The only distinction between these two very opposing meanings is the vowel under the "shin" "ש." The negative meaning has only the vowel "־" where the positive also has a "vav" "ו." The difference between feeling alive and feeling the opposite is the support of being part of something.

Each one of us is a different letter that reflects God's image. If a Torah is missing even one letter, it is invalid and can not be used. If even one person is missing, we as a people, as humanity, are incomplete and God's glory is diminished. May we support and expand the walls of God's house to make this world a welcoming place for all of us and God.

RABBINIC FAILURES

CORRUPTION AND GREED GET IN THE WAY OF THE TORAH[44]

Since I became observant in high school, I've been asked, "How can religious people act that way?" by non-Orthodox friends and family more than I would like to remember — and sometimes they are asking a good question.

I have had the privilege of spending the decade after high school in full-time learning in two of the largest yeshivas in the world, one in Lakewood, New Jersey, and one in Jerusalem. Sitting in a room with 800 other young men, learning, speaking, and breathing the texts that have been part of our tradition for 3,500 years, the Torah looks alive and very well.

Yesterday I saw several of those young men being arrested by the FBI for fraud. We were taught to be *talmidei chachamim* — practitioners of the Torah's wisdom. The goal was to minimize, and ideally eliminate, the space between the ideal Torah-centric life and the actual way we live our lives.

Unfortunately, the void between the two is vast and painfully disappointing, and continues to widen. The world and our communities are changing, perhaps faster than ever, but spiritual practice is often frozen in time. There is complex tension between innovation and tradition that requires collective rabbinic skill to address. But instead of

---

[44] Originally published n June 27, 2017 as "In Lakewood, Sometimes Corruption And Greed Get In The Way Of The Torah" by the *Forward*

being present for the holy labor of asking what God expects from us now, the pause button was pressed and the need for updated answers avoided.

The Torah has tragically been placed in a rabbinically induced solipsistic coma at the very time that we need it to be awakened. It's hard to know the exact year that the government started to be perceived as the enemy of the yeshiva community, but based on the posture in our community toward women, I would guess before 1920. Having never seen Hebrew grammar or the Prophets on the syllabi of any yeshiva speaks to the range of post-enlightenment education that is lacking in our schools.

I have heard stories of young couples giving money to an uncle, with a different last name, to use as a down payment on a house. Then the couple would live there while the government (and its taxpayers) were paying their mortgage. Rumors of second-party checks being used as currency had made their way to the coffee rooms in Israel. Still, I was not prepared for the dominance of this culture of Lakewood.

My first encounter with systemic corruption was, sadly, at the local Jewish bookstore. The rabbi rang up the books, but the price changed when I took out my debit card. Unfamiliar with the custom of the city, I asked, "Is it a different price for cash and credit?" "No," he said, "I just need to charge you tax if there is a record of it." Unfortunately, this was only the beginning.

The system is broken and it starts at the top. I tell the following story with a very heavy heart. It involves a rabbi that was kind to me. He inspired me and honored us with naming our son. This rabbi once told me that people are like *borer*, the act of separating on Shabbos: You have to take the good from the bad. It is with that intention that I share this reflection because there is also much good in Lakewood.

Everyday, I opened the *frum*, or religious, gym at 5:30 a.m. and worked as a personal trainer before yeshiva started. When I got the job, the owner asked me how I wanted to be paid. "The 1st and 15th?" I answered, not really understanding the question. "No. Do you want me to pre-tithe it for you?" He then explained how there was a wonderful outreach organization that would give him back 90% of a monthly "donation" he made to them in cash. He would get a deduction, no one would have to pay taxes or declare it as income, the organization could continue its "holy work" and I wouldn't have to tithe it (i.e. give 10% of it to charity).

I was silent with disgust, and then it got worse. "Ask a *shailah*," he said. "Everyone does it." Out of curiosity, I called my local *posek*, or decisor. "Cheat!" he ruled with enthusiasm, as if it were a mitzvah.

I did not. It is the Torah, God, and the world that are being cheated. How can the choice between being ethical or following the rabbis even exist at all?

When *da'at*, or the opinion of, Torah is said by rabbis who are living in a time and among people who do not acknowledge the reality of the world that the rest of us experience, they are answering a question rather than the person. It could be that the answer is the correct one, if asked under unrecognizably different circumstances in a time and land far, far away.

I later asked the renowned *Mashgiach* of the yeshiva, Rabbi Salomon, how it is that those not in yeshiva, and even those who don't have a spiritual practice, seem to be doing a much better job at the things that we are meant to take most seriously.

Until the Torah gets to respond, in present tense, the question will remain better than the answer.

ORTHODOX JEWS AND THE CHILD VICTIMS ACT[45]

While learning in the Mir Yeshiva in Jerusalem, my study partner and I attended a lecture from the great Jewish thinker, Rabbi Moshe Shapiro. Later that week, we saw him at the Western Wall praying at sunrise. My friend asked him a question on the lecture he had given earlier in the week. Rabbi Shapiro responded: "If you don't understand this, then there is a lot you don't understand!"

This answer sums up my feelings on the religious right's response to the Child Victims Act, and other recent positions. How can we take their statements against women's ordination seriously when they have so grossly misappropriated their own role as rabbis? If you can't understand that it is wrong to stand with child molesters and the institutions that have long protected and enabled them, how can we not question what else you don't understand?

In our daily prayers, we ask God to "restore our judges as in earliest times and our counselors as at first; remove from us sorrow and groan; and reign over us — You, God, alone - with kindness and compassion, and justify us through judgment." This blessing is one of the twelve (original) blessings in the middle of the Amidah, the prayer that is central to every service. The Zohar explains that these twelve blessings relate to the twelve tribes, and

---

[45] Originally published on February 13, 2018 as "Why On Earth Are Orthodox Jews Opposing The Child Victim's Act?" by the *Forward*

the tradition teaches that this blessing corresponds to the tribe of Naftali.

Naftali was the last tribe, in the formation of the encampment around the portable tabernacle in the wilderness, and was responsible for making sure that no one got left behind and thereby became vulnerable. In the early mystical work Book of Creation, Adar - the last month of the year, corresponds to Naftali. The stone on the ancient priestly breastplate representing the tribe of Naftali is the שבו (*shavu*), agate, which also alludes to a return, שב (*shuv*). Tradition teaches that the month of Adar has the potential to turn things around, just like in the Purim story. This year needs to be different.

At this time last year, I stood with survivors in Albany, and listened to each one tell their horrific story of abuse to legislators. One of the men, in his fifties and in tears, said that he was so envious that I still had faith in God. He lost his in the rectory with his priest. I felt so powerless to stop the additional trauma these individuals suffer knowing that many of those predators are still out there preying on innocent children. Yet, something can be done to bring justice for many whose lives are forever altered by changing New York's statutes of limitations - one of the shortest in the country.

I don't understand why the interfaith work of some is limited to forming alliances to protect abusers. I can't understand why the faith and safety of so many is worth trading to protect the funds of the few and evil. I want to understand why there is constant conversation about protecting the power of those who have it and complete silence when it comes to protecting those abused by it.

On February 27, the day before Purim, I will return to the State Senate to lobby with others in support of the Child Victims Act. Please join in restoring the moral voice of faith leaders to protect children and support survivors by contacting your representatives and religious organizations to encourage them to vote for this bill.

TEXTUAL ACTIVISM

There are things which are complicated and hard to understand. This isn't one of them.

HEALING THE AFFLICTIONS OF SEPARATION[46]

The Talmud teaches (Megillah 31b): "If old men advise you to demolish, and children [advise you] to build, then demolish and do not build, because the demolishing of old men is [as constructive] as building and the building of children is demolishing." In other words: wise elders can help us see when it's time to demolish old structures, practices, and ideas that no longer serve — so that the demolishing becomes the first step toward building something new.

I just returned from a trip to the United States / Mexico border co-sponsored by HIAS and T'ruah: the Rabbinic Call for Human Rights. We visited the Otero County Processing Center, which houses over 1000 migrants who have been separated from their families. The refugees housed there have not committed any crime, but the warden referred to them as "inmates." They wore colored jumpsuits, and slept 50 to a room behind bars. These family separations are connected with the affliction described in this week's *parsha* — and in the Torah's cure for that affliction, we can find tools to heal and to build.

Rashi writes, on Leviticus 14:4, "since the affliction [of *tzara'as*] comes about because of *lashon ha-ra* (malicious speech) which is an act of verbal twittering, therefore for purification Torah requires birds that constantly twitter." *Tzara'as* isn't (just) a skin condition: it's a moral condition, rooted in the sin of malicious speech.

---

[46] Originally published on April 7, 2019 by the Bayit Builder's Blog

In another interpretation, the Talmud (Arakhin 15b) explains that the word "*metzora*" (a person with *tzara'as*) can be understood in the language of "*motzi ra*," giving off evil. *Metzora* is when a person's essence becomes so twisted that whatever that person says or does is bad.

Our rabbis also say that this affliction of *tzara'as* comes from arrogance. For this reason, Rashi explains, the Torah prescribes a cure of cedarwood, crimson wool, and hyssop. "What is the remedy so that one should be cured? He should lower himself from his arrogance like a worm [תולעת / *tola'at* means both wool and worm] and like hyssop [which grows low to the ground]." And why cedar? According to the Midrash (Tanchuma 3) the cedar's tall magnificence reminds us that the sinner thought of themselves as glorious (and needs to adjust their self-image a bit).

The Talmud (Sotah 5a) teaches us that God separates from us when we are arrogant — something that doesn't happen with any other character trait. Our purpose in life is to see God as the source of all, and not fill space with the fake reality that we are somehow better than any other person created by God. When we are arrogant, God pulls away from us. When our eyes are open, we recognize that in our connectedness with each other, we experience connectedness with God… and when we separate from each other, we separate from God.

The family separations that I witnessed on the border are horrific examples of this profanity. Not only are parents and children separated from each other, but all who take part in creating and enforcing that separation are maintaining a system that separates us from God.

The rehabilitation of the *metzora*, as described in the Torah, involves experiencing a temporary separation from community (Leviticus 14:3). We can see that as a kind of sensitivity training. If *tzara'as* is (as Rashi and the Talmud teach) an affliction of arrogance and malicious speech, then the *metzora* needs time away from community to do their own work so that they can return with a sense of the communal responsibility that must be at the core of all spiritual practice. Every sin between people creates separation between us and God. We need to build in a way that heals that separation — and heals our illusory sense of separateness from each other, too.

As builders of the Jewish future, we must turn away from *lashon ha-ra* (wicked speech). We must turn away from the temptation of arrogance or holding ourselves to be separate from or better than others. All of these are today's *tzara'as* — a word that shares its root with *tzuris*, suffering. Wicked speech, arrogance, and separating ourselves from each other - are our *tzara'as* and our *tzuris* — and these are no way to build.

The rabbis opine that the two birds slaughtered at the start of this week's *parsha* (Leviticus 14:4) can represent two approaches to building a more humble and human society. One path is to first focus on the greatness of God and all of God's wonders, which helps us more accurately calibrate our own greatness. Alternatively, we can start by looking at the loneliness of the human experience. What's behind our capacity as a people to create terrible separations like those unfolding at the US/Mexico border? Examining that, we should see clearly that the places and policies that come out of *lashon ha-ra*, arrogance, and separation need to be demolished.

The Torah gives us tools: tackling our twittering (let spring's birdsong remind us to sing the greatness of God, not to speak wickedness or untruths), cultivating humility (hinted-at by the wool and the low-growing hyssop), and recalibrating our sense of awe (remembering the majestic cedar). With these we can demolish old structures that serve to separate, and we can build something holy in their place.

INTERFAITH

INTERFAITH LEADERS STAND UP FOR YES ON 3 CAMPAIGN[47]

There is a myth that has circulated for years that the things that make us different actually make a difference. Our race, religion, culture, gender, sexuality, and everything in between are markers of worth created and cultivated to separate. The myth of difference and the expectation that faith leaders not only adhere to but promote its perceived value, is fundamentally toxic and subversive.

A referendum on this November's ballot seeks to legalize the dehumanization of transgender people by removing protections against discrimination in public places. By supporting the people of Massachusetts to vote Yes on 3, we are affirming our belief that every individual is deserving of dignity and fair treatment. As faith leaders, our commitment to voting Yes on 3 is directly influenced by our understanding of God's call to each of us through scripture and prayerful discernment of how God wants us to see and support each other.

Looking specifically at the multiple branches of Judaism and Christianity, we can deconstruct the myth of difference through the common thread that unites us all: we are created by God. When we see the world and each other through the lens of the creation story found in our shared sacred text, the book of Genesis, it's clear that our creation and existence are intrinsically equitable. What we

---

[47] Originally published on October 31, 2018 by *Medium*, co-authored with Reverend Stephanie Kendell.

designate as difference is actually an expansive view of God's desire to create humanity in unique ways and yet equally the same. Our differences, especially when we come together in community, help us to see and experience a more complete understanding of the One who created us.

The Genesis narrative teaches us that God created everything and declared it good. "Plants and trees, each after its kind. All living things that crawl, and swim in the sea, each after its kind. And all winged fowl, of every kind." However, the phrase "of its kind" is omitted when humankind is created because there are not different kinds of people. There are no footnotes or caveats that make certain individuals exceptions to the rule that all people are created by and are a direct reflection of God. It is not only faithful to God to recognize transgender people as created good and whole, but sacrilegious to make these unholy distinctions of discrimination. Supporting policies and laws that help us keep our trans community visible, valued, and safe is also necessary as part of spiritual practice!

When God creates a transgender person, they are thoughtfully made, seen, and called good just like Adam and Eve, who transitioned from being one person to two. God is not limited by human imagination or understanding and can create infinite variations of the same thing. Every part of us is created with intention. There are no exceptions. It is the same for each and every one of us, no matter how uniquely God created you, or how society has labeled you as different. For Christians and Jews this is the crux of our understanding the Divine: A God that is wildly creative, meticulously imaginative, and perfectly intentioned. A God that created all humans in God's likeness, without exception.

Using God to divide people rather than connecting them is a sin. As faith leaders we must name and work to dismantle all sinful structures of power. Supporting homophobia is sin. Transphobia is sin. White supremacy is a sin. Oppression of any sort is sin. Please help elevate the truest identity of all people, of all divine creations, by voting YES on 3 and supporting trans equality and human dignity.

THE AUDACIOUS AND INSPIRATIONAL GIFT OF PRIDE[48]

A prominent progressive faith leader posted a question on Facebook this week asking other faith leaders and scholars, "How are you doing with everything that is going on politically?" This has been a week in which all of us are feeling the deep divisions in our country.

Those of us who inhabit spaces of privilege may feel a growing hopelessness, like a chasm opening up in front of us these days; it's like the advent of a deep nighttime that perhaps we have not seen before. We are waking up to the realities of injustice and oppression that have defined the daily lived experience of too many of our neighbors. For those of us who tend faith communities and teach people of faith how to birth into the world more kindness, justice, and peace, well…times are hard.

Folks answered the question with comments like:

"I'm angry, really angry, and when not angry, deeply depressed."

"I kind of lost my composure in preaching class today. I'm the professor."

"I'm tired and worried."

"Pretty scatterbrained and struggling to focus. My sleeping is erratic."

"Exhausted."

"I felt physically ill driving to the office this morning, and realized it was a physical reaction to the

---

[48] Originally published on June 21, 2018 by *Tikkun,* co-authored with Reverend Amy Butler

news I was listening to."

"Helpless to change the situation."

Any one of us paying even the slightest attention to the atrocious policies being implemented by the American government, both within, along, and outside our borders, can't be unfamiliar with feelings like these. Sometimes the darkness of this world, the evil all around us, steals our joy and compromises our resolve.

Yet we know, especially those of us who speak from a religious platform, that we must keep speaking, we must keep calling for love and justice, we must insist on welcoming the light, or evil will even co-opt religion, as it has over and over again. How can we keep going?

It's Pride month. All across the country people of many faith expressions and no faith expression are celebrating the full inclusion of LGBTQ people in our communities. There's light where there was none before, a world in which new generations of LGBTQ young people will be loved and accepted exactly as they are. It has taken us long enough to affirm their status as beloved children of God, and still they struggle to enjoy the same full rights as others...but, oh what a long way we have come.

God's first creative act, "Let there be light" models for us how we are meant to respond to darkness in the world: we are to make light. In the oppressive, incapacitating, and depressing darkness of hate, discrimination, and inequality we have witnessed the hope-filled joy of LGBT Pride.

It was June 28, 1969 when Pride began with a riot at The Stonewall Inn in New York City. Like most gay bars in the '50s and '60s, Stonewall was a sanctuary where people who had to hide their identities (or face socially sanctioned bigotry if they couldn't), could fully embrace their humanity and the image of God they represent. Many have noted that Stonewall in particular was a safe haven for the most marginalized of the LGBTQ community – drag queens, transgender persons, and others who did not conform to gender stereotypes. And when the forces of oppression sought to raid this safe haven, the most marginalized of society responded by shining their light, by boldly declaring that they will not be ashamed of who God created them to be, and by expanding spaces of sanctuary into more and more corners of our society. One spark catching fire.

For more than 50 years Stonewall has been a beacon of hope that has created community, progress, and sustainable optimism – in fabulous ways! The LGBTQ community has refused to be silenced by societal oppression or even content with stasis after the considerable achievements of marriage equality and adoption rights. These gains are now being threatened and the legalization of discrimination, based on gender or sexual identity, is a real danger.

As religious leaders, we are often asked some version of the theological question "Why doesn't God feed the hungry, heal the sick, and protect the vulnerable?" Jewish tradition holds a concept that we are to be partners with God in the healing of the world. If the world was perfect, how would we contribute? Darkness can only exist in the absence of light, but without the darkness there wouldn't be a need for light. Christian scriptures read: "The light shines in the darkness, and the darkness has not overcome it."

There is so much work to be done and it is really hard to look at this world and not get depressed. The situation in which we're living is indeed exhausting, draining, and often overwhelming. But God forbid it should ever be easier to be motivated to do something about it.

This weekend let's take to the streets with our LGBTQ friends and be nourished and reinvigorated as we celebrate: being created in God's image; being loved for who we are; keeping hope for a changed future alive; shining light, even just a little, until every corner of this world shines with welcome and hope.

OPENING DOORS AND HEARTS ON TRANSGENDER DAY OF VISIBILITY[49]

Religious communities are places where we gather to tell our stories within the context of a Divine narrative – the story of God. In theory, we can show up with every part of who we are at our churches, synagogues and mosques – beloved creations of a God who loves us more than we could possibly understand. And when we create these kinds of sanctuaries, we learn to live in community with people who understand themselves and us as such.

People of faith believe that communities like that can change the world. Sounds great, right?

Most of us want to say that our religious communities are places like this, but the truth is that members of the transgender community often do not feel this kind of safety and welcome – often and maybe even especially in communities of faith.

Statistics tell us that in the United States approximately one person in 100 does not identify with the binary gender they were assigned at birth. That means it's statistically very likely there is someone in the orbit of your faith community who is a member of the transgender community; it might even be a family member who is too afraid to tell you.

Think about your own faith community: could a person of transgender experience show up and join in with

---

[49] Originally published on March 26, 2019 as "Transgender Day: a chance for churches to open doors and hearts to our transgender neighbors" by *Baptist News,* co-authored with Reverend Amy Butler

every part of who they are, celebrated for their story as part of the Divine narrative?

A Divine narrative – the story of God – by its very definition defies our complete understanding, so as people of faith we have to do the humble work of admitting that we are not always aware of holiness even when it is right in front of us. Genesis 28:16 reads, "Jacob awoke from his sleep and said 'Surely God is in this place and I did not know!'" In Hebrew, the last letter of the first four words spells "community." Perhaps that reference invites us, within our own faith communities, to look toward those whom society places last and to amplify those voices if our aim is really to create holy community, a reflection of God's love for the world.

When you can't find acceptance or even just visibility in a community of people who claim to worship the Divine when they gather, it is easy to mistake the opinions and actions of people for the judgment of God. And, as we know, the results of that can be devastating. Nearly 50 percent of transgender people who do not find acceptance and affirmation by those close to them attempt to end their own lives, God forbid. Religious communities, in our inability and unwillingness to see and affirm transgender people, number among those who contribute to the pain, suffering, and death of this community.

This is not what God intended; it is not approved, endorsed, allowed, or supported by the will of the Divine.

In fact, as our society begins to make advances in understanding and supporting the transgender experience, religious communities must become leaders in creating spaces where transgender people openly and gladly tell their stories and are celebrated as the beautiful parts of God's creation that they are.

Congregations, it's past time to open your doors and your hearts to your transgender neighbors.

And, clergy, it's up to us to lead the way.

Pastor Amy:

Our congregation is blessed with a family whose 11-year-old daughter recently transitioned. We've walked with them, and her, through this painful and beautiful process. As this family endured all the challenges of adjusting at school and among friends and family, one more transition loomed on the immediate horizon. That fall Sally would prepare to participate in her first Christmas pageant as her true self. She had played many roles before, but this year would be different.

The criteria for playing Mary, a central character in the play, was pretty rigorous. The child in the role of Mary had to commit to regular and frequent rehearsals; she had to agree to memorize all the lines – no scripts allowed; and she had to be a member of the oldest children's class in the Sunday school. The one child who qualified and wanted the part most was Sally, our transgender child.

It was critically important that we see and affirm her by casting her in this role, and we did. That decision sent an important message to the congregation and an important message to Sally and her family: when we say that all people are seen and welcomed in this community, we mean it.

Rabbi Mike:

I was asked by a young couple to officiate their wedding and help with assigning the various honors. Between the time they invited me to officiate and the date of the wedding, the flower girl transitioned to a boy and still wanted to keep that role in the wedding. I met with the couple and asked, "How do you feel about having a flower boy?" They were thrilled, so I took him to buy his first suit.

The couple helped that boy feel seen and affirmed, and their decision sent a message to the whole community that the identities and life cycle events of all people are holy.

When we people of faith tell the story of creation, we share a narrative of the Divine modeling limitless diversity in all its beauty and calling it good. Those of us who tend sacred spaces, tell sacred stories, and nurture sacred community should be the first to honor the stories and identities of transgender people in our communities. We do that best when we reach out a hand and say clearly for all to hear, "I see you. God loves you. You are welcome here. Come in and tell your story."

March 31 is the international Transgender Day of Visibility, founded in 2009. The congregations we serve are planning programming to help their communities engage this conversation.

FAITH LEADERS MUST STOP ACTING AS IF THERE'S NO PREVENTING NATURAL DISASTERS[50]

Hurricanes have been in the news a lot lately. A lot. And with every storm comes another litany of lives lost — each one a child of God — and destruction to the planet that many of our faith traditions teach we are to steward and protect.

Most recently, Hurricane Ophelia, the easternmost Atlantic hurricane on record, battered Ireland and the United Kingdom. Most of the people who died during this storm didn't die from the impacts of floods or collapsing homes, but because of the wildfires fueled by the winds of the hurricane.

This comes after the deadliest wildfires in California history, which claimed at least 40 lives, and which forced the evacuation of 90,000 people from their homes. In the last two months alone, Hurricanes Harvey, Irma, and Maria have unleashed unprecedented destruction on the inhabitants of Texas, Florida, Puerto Rico, and the U.S. Virgin Islands, with the Caribbean Island of Barbuda declared "practically uninhabitable" by its prime minister, Gaston Browne. Gone. Wiped from the map.

In the midst of ever more surreal headlines, the phrases become routine, like so much of the dysfunction and suffering currently affecting our nation: we hear only about the deadliest, the hottest, the most expensive on

---

[50] Originally published on November 3, 2017 by *Religion News Service,* co-authored with Reverend Amy Butler

record.

We jump into action after destruction has hit with courageous self-sacrifice and awe-inspiring generosity, all the while pretending as if there was nothing we could do before the storm hit, before the fires started.

As faith leaders, we believe it's time we stopped pretending and summoned our great generosity of spirit and incalculable ingenuity to address the ongoing disaster that is causing so many of our other disasters: climate change.

In the last several decades, natural disasters have been increasing in both frequency and intensity. And 40 percent of the world's population, including our fellow New Yorkers, live on coastlines while sea levels are rising.

Last weekend (Oct. 28) New Yorkers from across our city marched to mark five years since Superstorm Sandy pounded the Eastern Seaboard, causing billions of dollars in damage, and devastating coastal New Jersey and New York City in particular.

In those five years, while some significant action has been taken to help residents recover and rebuild, many of our fellow New Yorkers still remain out of their homes. And there has been very little action to prevent the next storm from hitting and not enough done fast enough to shore up our neighborhoods from that next storm and sea level rise.

With the current federal administration pulling us out of the most aggressive and comprehensive global plan to combat climate change, the Paris Agreement, the need for New York to be the climate champion that acts is greater than ever.

In the past it has often been pointed out that although the United States is one of the largest global producers of carbon emissions and consumers of energy, we are also the most insulated from the detrimental impacts of changing climates. Our wealth and infrastructure enable us to adapt. Meanwhile, it is the world's poorest populations that have contributed the least to climate change who are hit the hardest by its effects, and are least able to recover.

This is all still true. And, after Sandy, and Irma, and Harvey, and Maria, and wildfires, and floods, can we really say that the U.S. is not being significantly impacted?

We are not climate scientists, or policy experts, or politicians. We deal with the aftermath of the failure of these groups to form consensus and have the political will to act. We are the ones who somehow have to comfort families who have lost everything, sometimes including a loved one. We hear the stories of all that cannot be rebuilt. It is our congregations that raise money for victims, assemble hurricane buckets, and send relief workers.

The climate crisis is a moral crisis and it will require moral courage to address it. But our faith teaches that we must not allow fear and a mentality of scarcity to drive us to inaction. That is why earlier this year The Riverside Church voted to divest from fossil fuels. We cannot remain invested in the very coal, oil, and gas companies that are most responsible for climate change. Our city and state must also cut its ties from these industries that are out of alignment with a healthy climate and thriving communities.

It is time we demand our elected leaders take further, deeper, morally justified, action to address climate change. Our world, our people, needs New York to be a beacon of hope that others can aspire to.

We cannot wait for another storm or fire or flood before we act.

FAITH IN THE FACE OF FEAR[51]

This week has been a difficult one for many. Initial anxiety at the undoing of so much progress towards equality was quickly validated by an increase in hate crimes and unbridled fear. It's just as easy to tell people to have faith as it is to be passive. But our religion is one of action. What does faith call upon us to do when we see ourselves in opposition to the dominant culture without an obvious action item to harness the objection?

In this week's Torah portion, Lech Le'cha, God comes to Abraham after the war with Sodom and tells him not to be afraid because God will protect him. Why did Abraham only express his fear after he had already successfully won the war? Earlier in this week's *parsha*, God says that Abraham will be a blessing. Abraham's blessing is emphasized by our tradition in the daily Amidah prayer:

מלך עוזר ומושיע ומגן. ברוך אתה ה' מגן אברהם. O King, Helper, Savior, and Shield. Blessed are You, Hashem, Shield of Abraham.

Even though the blessing starts with all three of our forefathers, Rashi notes that only Abraham's name is invoked at its conclusion. Abraham is known to represent *chesed*, or kindness, as Isaac symbolizes prayer and service, and Jacob represents Torah. These are the three pillars on which the world stands. In ending this blessing with Abraham, we emphasize kindness as the attribute most

---

[51]Originally delivered as a drashah on November 12, 2016 at the Old Broadway Synagogue

worthy of divine protection.

    This blessing also lists three attributes of God: עוזר ומושיע ומגן, the King that helps, saves, and shields. Our rabbis tell us that these three salvific acts correspond to three levels of faith. In all three cases, a person tries to do the right thing, but the environment and level of difficulty differs. The first dynamic, עוזר (helps), is when a person puts in the effort to be successful and hopes that God will assist them in that pursuit. The next level, ומושיע (saves), is when a person is passive towards achieving the goal, but they believe that God will save them. The third, ומגן (shields), is that in the pursuit of doing the right thing they put themselves in danger and rely on God to shield and protect them.

    We see these relationships reflected in three of Abraham's tests. In the first, God tells Abraham to go from his homeland without telling him where he will end up. Abraham has faith, does his part, and God helps out. When Abraham gets to the land of Israel, he confronts a second test: famine. Abraham does not know how to act to achieve salvation from hunger, but God directs him to Egypt and provides food. Finally, when it comes to saving Lot, Abraham puts himself in danger to fight his enemies and God shields him.

    If Abraham had already won the war against Sodom, why is the promise of protection given only after the fact? Our tradition teaches us that Abraham was in need of divine reassurance after seeing that the people of Sodom were not receptive to the ideas that he had fought for, such as love and emulating God's goodness. He was now going to have to be a constant voice of opposition against the selfishness and hatefulness of Sodom. How would he be able to maintain an unending front of kindness against a mighty and evil nation?

    This, I believe, is the blessing of the shield of Abraham. Abraham's legacy is one of perseverance: like Abraham, we are empowered to do what is right, stay strong in the face of fear, and to speak the truth of peace and righteousness. This act of faith itself merits divine protection as reward for following in God's path of spreading love and respect for humanity.

The mystics explain that Rashi's insight on the above blessing "with you [Abraham] they conclude and not with them" as a reference to the era of our later generations. We live in a time without the holy Temple and therefore our prayers and worship are not the same. Unfortunately, the Torah of our times isn't at all comparable to those who came before us. However, there is no excuse for us not to be as kind, generous, or compassionate as our ancestors were. We must proudly carry and expand this shield to help, save, and protect anyone who feels threatened, by imitating God and fighting against apathy. Let us have the faith to act and never be afraid to fight hate.

SPEECHES AND INTERVIEWS

HOMOPHOBIA IN ORTHODOXY[52]

I would like to share some thoughts and observations today about homophobia in Orthodox Judaism, in light of the hypocritical and offensive treatment of comedian Leah Forster.

God is not homophobic.

Homophobia is not part of our Jewish tradition.

In fact, if anything, the Torah seems to be preoccupied with heterophobia... A man and a woman aren't even allowed to be alone together, because it might lead to heterosexual acts outside of marriage. Even casual, platonic touching is avoided, lest it lead to heterosexual touching.

The Torah draws these lines to help guide us towards being in a healthy relationship with God. We also draw lines, but unfortunately these are often socially motivated and constructed to make us feel better about the way in which we choose to live our lives, and have little to do with God at all.

It's also not new.

Abraham told Sarah to say that she was his sister, because he would be killed if they knew she was really his wife. They were particular about adultery, but not murder. They also claimed it to be holy and about God. But if they really cared about God they wouldn't be killing husbands in order to marry their wives.

---

[52] Originally published on December 17, 2018 as a video titled "G-d is Not Homophobic" on Congregation Beit Simchat Torah's Facbeook page

Because we all speak *lashon ha-ra* - gossip and slander - we can have a global initiative to commit to an hour a day to not speak badly about other people, and feel good about the other 23 hours, when we are less particular.

Perhaps designating one hour to talk how we want to, and to really be careful the rest of the day, like we are supposed to, would be 23 times better. But we can't actually say that it's ok, rather we tell ourselves enough just to take the edge off of feeling bad, without really having to sacrifice for the good.

I'm from Virginia and there are folks there who really love their guns. They hold sacred the constitution, and see the 2nd amendment as spiritual practice. But when it comes to the 14th amendment, and immigration… well, let's say some are less devout. Because, in truth, it was never about the constitution, but rather people's desire to have guns.

If you are willing to say "Good Shabbos" to someone coming from the parking lot on Saturday morning, even though their Shabbos practice differs from yours, why aren't you're willing to say "mazel tov" to two men getting engaged, just because you see their marriage as different than yours?

If your synagogue offers a family membership to heteronormative couples that only had a civil marriage or a religious ceremony, where the woman also gives the man a ring which isn't seen as halachic by many, why wouldn't you provide that membership to married couples that happen to be gay?

If you are complicit in the celebration of criminals, like Rubashkin, who transgressed the Torah's prohibition of dishonesty in business, which is also called a *toa'veh*, an abomination, but protest the other march that occurs in June, it's not only homophobic, but it's also really inconsistent with Torah values and I encourage you to stop it.

Why, when a prominent Orthodox psychologist, who

was the leading expert and most vocal proponent of conversion therapy, was himself recently exposed trolling the internet for sex with men, isn't there a call to strive for truth and a new conversation about how to best respond to the frum LGBTQ population.

For kashrut agencies to be silent when they supervise horrific violations of worker rights, animal welfare, and other illegal activities, but feel obligated to advocate for straight only space, we have to question, what exactly are they being paid to observe?

There is only one Torah and it needs to be restored and purged of homophobia, transphobia, racism, misogyny, and all of the hateful things that were not given at Mt. Sinai. If these offensive things make you feel better about yourself, or your place in society, it says a lot about you, but nothing about Judaism.

To our LGBTQ siblings: while your sexual orientation isn't a choice, your religious identity is. Many in Orthodoxy have given you good reasons to want to leave. Please don't let the hate and ignorance win. We need you. We want you. We love you.

RESPONDING TO TRANS ERASURE[53]

It has been a hard few days as we have heard about this administration's desire to deny the identities of approximately 1.5 million Americans of trans experience. God forbid that it should ever be easier for us to be motivated to do something about it. I would like to share an insight that helps me cope by trying to effect change.

In this week's Torah portion, Va'yera, which means to be seen, we learn about the sole incident that is recorded in the Hebrew Bible about Abraham inviting guests. It is noteworthy for two reasons. The first is that the guests turn out to be angels that don't actually have an inherent need to be fed or welcomed. And the second is that the opportunity only came about because of Abraham's desire to fulfill the mitzvah couldn't come about through people because it was exceedingly hot that day and therefore no one was traveling. And so the rabbis ask that ostensibly, the obligation of inviting guests exists when there are people needing a place to go. So what was Abraham really accomplishing by taking care of angels that didn't actually need his help at all?

Our rabbis tell us that Abraham lived in a time that was in many ways very similar to ours. A time of inequality, a time of discrimination, and a time of oppression. And he wanted to model to the universe that all are welcome and all are seen; despite differences.

---

[53] Originally published on October 22, 2018 as a video titled "Rabbi Mike Moskowitz shares thoughts on trans equality" on Congregation Beit Simchat Torah's Facebook page

It is not coincidental that the word *"va'yera,"* to see is also the word for fear. Because it is so easy to be afraid of things that we have never experienced and people that we have never met. To such an extent that it can easily descend into hate. We have a responsibility and a holy charge to shift the climate of fear of experiences beyond our own, to a posture of radical inclusivity to create space for people to be seen for who they are.

For many people involved in trans advocacy, it's personal. What Abraham was trying to teach to people of all faiths is that you don't need to know someone to be able to feel their pain. Recognizing the increase of the pain and suffering of 1.5 million trans folks in America is something that we must all feel.

People of all faiths and good conscience can not be complicit in a society that wants to deny or erase the identity of human beings.

Our rabbis tell us that the best way to combat these microaggressions is by being proactive and try to commit and perform micro-affections.

The inviting guests of today must expand to create inviting spaces for people to be seen as who they are. As we think about the people in our lives who are in pain right now, it is so important to reach out. To those who we don't know personally we must especially reinvest and commit to change the dominant culture so that all are free to live without these threats. May we, like Abraham, bring light and love into the world by inviting people in as part of our spiritual practice.

RELIGIOUSLY NON-CONFORMING – UNORTHODOX PODCAST[54]

This past summer, Rabbi Mike Moskowitz became the first Orthodox rabbi to serve at the world's largest LGBTQ synagogue, Congregation Beit Simchat Torah, in Manhattan, where he is the Scholar-in-Residence in Trans and Queer Jewish Studies. Rabbi Moskowitz has long supported the LGBTQ community and trans inclusiveness in particular. At the time of his appointment, he spoke about his journey in supporting the LGBTQ community on the podcast Unorthodox, created by Tablet magazine. A lightly edited transcript of his interview with Unorthodox hosts Stephanie Butnick and Liel Leibovitz follows here.

Liel Leibovitz: So here's the thing. When someone imagines the rabbi they might meet in the world's largest LGBTQ synagogue, they don't imagine a dude looking like you, with a black hat and a beard. They don't imagine a traditional Orthodox rabbi. Tell us about the path that got you here.

Rabbi Mike Moskowitz: The path here was actually a very traditional rabbinic trajectory. I was a rabbi of Columbia University, with Aish New York. I was the rabbi of the Old Broadway Synagogue, which is an Orthodox synagogue, right by JTS [the conservative Jewish Theological Seminary]. And I had transgender congregants and a trans student at Columbia that was really struggling.

---

[54] Originally aired on June 14, 2018 on Tablet's *Unorthodox* podcast

And as a rabbi of a synagogue in Harlem, it's a pretty diverse and progressive space, all things considered.

As I started to meet more transfolks and started to create a space that was trans inclusive, I recognized that I was in a unique position to try to provide some scaffolding to support the trans Jewish experience, so people shouldn't have to choose between a gender identity and a religious identity.

Leibovitz: As you embarked on that mission, I imagine that there were some people in your community who looked at your work and said, "Why are you doing this?" It's highly, if I may, unorthodox. Did you face a lot of struggle going through that?

Rabbi Moskowitz: Internally I did not find any sort of struggle. There was a kind of an invitation to be a light in the darkness where other people weren't. So personally I found a level of clarity and comfort in knowing that I felt like I was doing the right thing. But from the outside there's still tremendous opposition daily, in the emails, on Facebook posts.

Leibovitz: Saying what?

Rabbi Moskowitz: Saying that these things are actually mutually exclusive. You can't be an orthodox rabbi and be supportive of the LGBTQ community. I wrote an article about marching with Pride that I really feel when so many marginalized segments of society are being targeted, that we as Jews have a responsibility to stand up, because we're also targeted as a minority. So the idea that somehow we can be passive or apathetic here -- like you have to choose sides. It's either about standing up for those who are the most vulnerable or recognizing that it's probably just a matter of time before we don't have the privilege and the entitlement and the agency to do something about it.

Leibovitz: How do you respond to someone who goes on Facebook and just angrily rants at you, "But you know being gay is not allowed in the Torah. It's halachically bad." [Halacha is Jewish law.] How do you square that? Because you see a lot of people in the Orthodox community who are very sensitive to these issues, but you really took a leadership stand on it.

Rabbi Moskowitz: Gender identity and sexual identity are very different. I think it's very easy to hate things that you don't know and it's really easy to kind of mush all this stuff you haven't been exposed to into one little space. So I think the first thing is to try to create space for dialogue, to try to recognize that the struggles of a gender identity are actually very different, both culturally and socially and also in Jewish law, from one of sexual identity. I deeply believe in the autonomy of each person's relationship with God, that it should be the result of our unique life experiences. If we can't create a safe space for people to be authentic and genuine about who they are in that relationship with God, then what is religion? It's not about me in intimacy with God. So the Torah says what the Torah says and everybody gets to figure out what that means for them as an individual. I think that there's a lot that we as Jews can learn from the trans world about being present in the moment, in the most authentic space and embracing a certain amount of fluidity in our relationship with God.

Stephanie Butnick: I'm curious. Given the sort of rigid differentiation between men and women in ultra-Orthodox spaces, how do LGBTQ issues arise in that world?

Rabbi Moskowitz: Within the gender space many people find it very affirming. For the trans experience to exist, there needs to be differences between men and women, or else there's no space to transition. So when one walks into an Orthodox synagogue you have to make a choice right away. What side of the mechitza [a partition used to separate men and women] do you want to sit on? Because there's so much gender-based spiritual practice for people who find that type of spiritual practice affirming, the challenge becomes one of providing the invitation and the resources to help the individual navigate all of those gendered choices in Orthodox synagogue, about being counted in a minyan [the minimum number of participants required, 10 men, for traditional Jewish public prayer], getting an Aliyah [being called up to the Torah], chevra kadisha [traditional performance of rites for the deceased] issues. There are all sorts of gender-based spiritual practices that make it a little bit more nuanced. Whereas in a more egalitarian space, in that area you don't have to make a choice but you also don't get the affirmation.

Butnick: It's interesting. When you call it affirming, I would imagine it can be very intense and frightening for someone for whom gender identity is sort of a question at a certain moment, to have to choose a side.

Rabbi Moskowitz: One of the things that is really complicated in the way in which Halacha creates a binary around male and female in certain kinds of halachic spaces -- doesn't necessarily resonate with people who adopt a gender non-conforming identity. And then it's complicated. Ideally a tri-chitza, right? [Leibovitz laughs, Rabbi Moskowitz is making a word play on mechitza basically referring to three genders] It allows for those who don't feel like they fit in the binary. I often speak about borrowing language from the queer community. That I was assigned secular, and then identified as ultra-Orthodox, and now I'm some version of religious non-conforming, and that kind of space to be able to be recognized in present tense where I am in a relationship with God allows for it to be much more alive and also conscious and deliberate. If every Jew would be as aware of their religious identity the way in which trans folks are about their gender identity, there'd be no apathy, there'd be no assimilation. It would just be a constant recognition.

Leibovitz: We would be on fire.

Rabbi Moskowitz: That's what we're looking for.

Leibovitz: You wrote a piece for Tablet that I found very moving about the importance of accepting people's choice of their own names and why that actually resonates sort of spiritually as well as civically.

Rabbi Moskowitz: In the Jewish tradition we believe that names are very powerful. That emanates from the power of speech. God said, "Let there be light," and there was. So this world was created through letters and we find this throughout the tradition. You can look at the article. There's a way in which transfolks in having to distill who they are in terms of an identity, especially if there's been a shift into a name, is often the most immediate point of entry in a conversation that either allows for a person to be rejected or accepted. And so when a person speaks about their pronouns and their name, it's not simple in the mind of a trans person. That's one of the reasons why I co-authored it with a transman, is to have it in that first person experience that "hello, my name is" is much more of an exposed experience where there's a posture of vulnerability and fragility for a trans person. So I think one of the things that's really important as an ally is to listen to that voice about the experiences that we have. "Hi. Are you Rabbi Moskowitz or are you Mike?" The stakes there aren't actually very high for me. I don't care. But for a trans person, it represents so much more of the way they're being seen.

Butnick: How does that play out within a Jewish context?

Rabbi Moskowitz: Some people choose a Jewish name or a Hebrew name. We have it within the tradition as something being very powerful. We have it deep within our tradition that if a person, God forbid, is sick, we add a name. Moses changes [Hosea's] name [to "Joshua"] in anticipation of an event. The Torah says that we can no longer call Abraham "Abram." We have to say the new name and not the old name. We find the struggle, it's literally in the struggle with the angel, that Jacob gets a name change from the individual to the communal [he becomes "Israel"] and the mystics that tell us that it was that moment where he went back for the pachim k'tanim -- the smallest, the most vulnerable, the most marginalized. So I think it's in this space of struggle where we try to create new space to uncover the divine will and it's in that place of the progressiveness of Halacha, which is the language of holacha, which means "to go" [also "to walk" or "the way to walk"], which is where the Talmud says God exists -- in this exile. It's in that place with God to explore and to expand in these new spaces. As the world continues to move, how can we allow the Torah to speak in present tense? In the Jewish tradition, a name really reflects the embodiment of being able to be present as one's fuller self.

Butnick: It seems like there is space even within religious Judaism for transfolk, for a questioning. It actually works well within the structure.

Rabbi Moskowitz: I think if we want for there to be space for Jews, then there needs to be space for trans Jews. Because one of those is a choice. Religion, and a religious identity, is an absolute choice of showing up and being present in that relationship with God. Gender identity, sexual identity, those aren't action items. Those are just identities. They just are. So if we force a person to choose, they will walk away from religion. So if we believe that God is everywhere all the time -- "Hashem [an expression for God, meaning "The Name," as Jews are not allowed to utter the name of God] is here. Hashem is there." So then what are we doing? We're just speaking to the reality that God is everywhere. And for each person there's the responsibility to ask the exact same question, "What does God want from me right now in this moment being who I am?" I don't think it gets more religious than that.

THE RABBINIC VOICE OF ALLYSHIP – HERE & NOW[55]

There's a widespread perception that fundamentalist faiths are incompatible with the LGBTQ identity. And for the most part, that's true — with a few exceptions.

Rabbi Mike Moskowitz is one of the few ultra-Orthodox Jewish rabbis who not only support, but actively advocate for, LGBTQ individuals. He tells Here & Now's Robin Young that despite his stand on these issues costing him his congregation and his job at Columbia University, he's proud of the work he now does with New York's Congregation Beit Simchat Torah.

"The rabbinic voice I don't think has been loud enough in creating a safe space," Moskowitz says. "That a sanctuary should be a sacred space, a sanctuary, from persecution. And unfortunately, religion now often excludes people."

Interview Highlights

On calling his choice to become an LGBTQ advocate a "holy decision"-

"I think we're all put in this world for a specific purpose, and for me, I've found clarity in the invitation to kind of expand the space that religion I think is meant to provide, as a container to help support relationships with God. There's just a huge segment of society that is being told, 'There's no room for you here,' and as a

---

[55] Originally aired on November 9, 2018 on WBUR's *Here & Now* as "This Ultra-Orthodox Rabbi Says His Holist Moment Was Becoming Public LGBTQ Ally"

fundamentalist, I believe that God is everywhere, all the time. We need some restorative religion to heal from some of the trauma that has been meted out by those who want to constrict the space that God occupies."

"I think that God isn't some sort of prefabricated, mass-produced space, and each person needs to ask themselves, 'What does God want from me, being who I am, in this relationship?'"

"The rabbinic voice I don't think has been loud enough in creating a safe space."

On what "ultra-Orthodox" means to him—

"I find it helpful to borrow language from the queer community about my own religious identity, because I think there's a huge parallel there. I was assigned secular, and then kind of came out as orthodox in high school, went on a right-wing trajectory for the next 20 years, learning in the largest seminaries in the world, and really living in that very far right-wing Lithuanian, yeshiva world. And now, [I] identify as religiously nonconforming. I have very progressive values, which are very much a part of who I am. I also am deeply religious."

"We all have to express ourselves with some sort of dominant physical form. And so for me, living in an ultra-Orthodox community, dressing the way in which rabbis in my community dress, is helpful in that it expresses to the world who I am at my core. If we force somebody to choose between a gender identity and a religious identity, or a sexual identity and a religious identity, there is only one out of those three which is a choice, and so people leave religion because they're told that there is no space for them to be who they are."

On this new "holy" understanding coming to him as a result of personal experience—

"Actually two different personal experiences that really led me in this quest to try to uncover and discover the divine will. First, someone in my family transitioned, and said, 'I'm not a girl, I'm a boy.' And that led me — I was a rabbi at Columbia University — to explore gender studies for the first time."

"And then when one of my students was really struggling as a trans individual, I felt a calling to really come out very publicly as an ally."

"When we have rabbis getting in between a person's relationship with God, it gets crowded. If a person is genuinely and sincerely on a quest to discover the divine intention, that struggle for truth is as holy as it gets."

On giving a speech on Hanukkah that he calls his "coming-out speech" about being an ally-

"For me, it felt so reminiscent of the feeling I had when I was 17, 20 years earlier, thinking about whether or not I was willing to take on the precarity of acknowledging the truth that I felt in my core to be absolute and objective, but was going to have consequences.... It was a similar struggle at 37, to come out again in that place of embarking on a journey to discover and uncover the divine will in a space that was very new for me. I think faith is a call to action, and when we're willing to do something in partnership with God for the greater good, and there's risks involved, I think that there's a way in which we manifest the divine will in the world of action."

On losing his job, and feeling isolated from the ultra-Orthodox community as a result of his advocacy-

"It's lonely and isolating, in that this space isn't occupied with other people with my background, and I think that's just the way it is when it comes to progress. But we also have some old truths that we can ground ourselves in, which are that God loves us more than we love ourselves, and God doesn't put extra people in this world and God so desperately yearns and longs to be in a relationship with each one of us. And unfortunately, the suicide rate among the trans community, for those who are not validated and affirmed, it's over 40 percent. Whether we understand the meta question of where gender lies is almost irrelevant, because we do understand the practical obligation to create a safe space for folks."

On whether the ultra-Orthodox community could shift further on LGBTQ issues-

"At the intersection of tradition and innovation, there is a lot of tension. If you change the rules too much, it's a different game. But if you don't adapt, no one's going to show up to play. And I think the far-right part of orthodoxy has drawn some lines with Sharpies, very permanent lines, but the problem is that that no longer fits the topography of the universe. And as rabbis, we're taught not to answer questions, but to answer people, and so the needs of people today are just different. So we don't need to change the tradition, but we need to recognize that its application to people needs to look different because people look different."

On what he says to people who say his advocacy is against God's will or an abomination-

"Nobody can ever own the relationship of another with God, and I think that we need to have much more autonomy given to the individual to own and take responsibility for our relationships with God. When we have rabbis getting in between a person's relationship with God, it gets crowded. If a person is genuinely and sincerely on a quest to discover the divine intention, that struggle for truth is as holy as it gets."

On arriving at this transcendent moment through meeting transgender people, and those words being similar-

"We find transitions deep within our tradition: from holiness to the mundane, from the day into the night. And sometimes it's a contradiction to the physical, because that plane of spirituality might look different than what we see with our physical eyes. Then if we have gendered aspects of God in our liturgy, 'Our father, our king,' and feminine aspects, and God doesn't have a body... where might gender lie, and what might that tell us about those who are able to sense things perhaps on a soul level?"

AGGADAH

ABOVE AND BELOW THE BINARY

God interacts with the world in a multitude of ways and yet is unified. So too, individuals present as opposing personality types but are in fact manifesting different aspects of God. Only by holding together the vast array of different human beings can we begin to appreciate the limitless nature of the Divine and reveal God's holiness in this world.

Even though Hillel and Shammai are presented as diametric opposites, they are both ultimate expressions of different aspects of God. This is an example of how in the physical sphere, people and traits appear very different, but in the spiritual realm they emanate from the same whole.

This essay intends to explore the relationship between the expression of a limited, dominant characteristic of unique individuality and the hidden expansiveness that contains the total collective. The focus will be on the Talmud's account of Hillel and Shammai as examples of spiritual practice that reflect the soul's source as a part within the whole.

Hillel's posture towards inclusivity and forgiveness is forged through a perspective of seeing the most essential aspect of every individual as that of being created in the image of God where God's glory is diminished by excluding those who want to come close. Hillel is motivated by love and understands God's desire to be emulated through unity, as God is one. He understands his relationship with God as akin to a parent and child. Hillel feels connected to others since he views them as siblings in God's family.

Shammai, by contrast, sees himself primarily as a servant of God and not as a son. This perspective allows

Shammai to be entirely focused on doing God's will. Shammai's own selfhood is irrelevant. His entire being is taken up with doing God's work, and as such he can be harsh with himself and others to ensure that his Master's will be perfectly carried out.

Starting with the most global perspective, we find a fundamental dispute between the study halls of Hillel and Shammai as to which was created first: the heaven or the earth[56].

> ת"ר ב"ש אומרים שמים נבראו תחלה ואח"כ נבראת הארץ
> שנאמר (בראשית א:א)"בראשית ברא אלקים את השמים
> ואת האר"ץ וב"ה אומרים
> ארץ נבראת תחלה ואח"כ שמים שנאמר (בראשית ב:ד)
> "ביום עשות ה' אלקים ארץ ושמים"
>
> Our Rabbis taught: Beit Shammai say: Heaven was created first and afterwards the earth was created, for it is said: In the beginning God created the heaven and the earth. Beit Hillel say: Earth was created first and afterwards heaven, for it is said: In the day that the Lord God made earth and heaven.

Although, there isn't any practical difference to the order for us, it does perhaps provide a frame and theme for other disputes. The order of candle lighting on Chanukah is a good first example[57].

> ת"ר מצות חנוכה נר איש וביתו והמהדרין נר לכל אחד
> ואחד והמהדרין מן המהדרין ב"ש אומרים יום ראשון מדליק
> שמנה מכאן ואילך פוחת והולך וב"ה אומרים יום ראשון

---

[56] חגיגה יב.

[57] שבת כא:

מדליק אחת מכאן ואילך מוסיף והולך אמר עולא פליגי בה תרי אמוראי במערבא ר' יוסי בר אבין ור' יוסי בר זבידא חד אמר טעמא דב"ש כנגד ימים הנכנסין וטעמא דב"ה כנגד ימים היוצאין וחד אמר טעמא דב"ש כנגד פרי החג וטעמא דבית הלל דמעלין בקדש ואין מורידין

    The Rabbis taught: The commandment of Chanukah is one light for a person and their household. And those who go after commandments should have one light for each person. And for those who are punctilious in pursuing commandments, Beit Shammai say on the first day one lights eight and then decreases one each day. But Beit Hillel say one lights one on the first day and then increases for the rest.

    Ulla said: Two Amoraim in Israel argue about this disagreement. R' Yose bar Avin and R' Yose bar Zevida. One said that Beit Shammai's reason is that they reference the days yet to come, and Beit Hillel's reason is in relationship to the days already passed. And one says that Beit Shammai's reason is that it correspond to the bull offerings of Sukkot, and Beit Hillel's reason is that we elevate in holiness and we do not lower.

Some commentators suggest that at the root of the dispute is the directionality of divine service[58]. Should a person begin, as Shammai opines, by focusing on the greatness of the Almighty in heaven and allow that to trickle down to make us more humble and minimize evil? Or should we start, as Hillel rules, with recognizing our own limitations and extend our goodness and holiness towards the heavens. It would seem that the goal of both

---

[58] באר משה פר' בראשית

opinions is to arrive at the same place but the question is from where to start.

There is a connection between Hillel and Shammai's opinions regarding the order of Creation, and their debate about the order of Chanukah candle-lighting. The School of Shammai holds that the Heavens were created first and so we begin our divine service with the maximum light of all eight candles. The light of these candles diminish and we remove one each night, much as human light diminishes as we move farther from the Heavens. The School of Hillel believes that the Earth was created first and then Creation moved Heavenward, much as the Chanukah candles begin on the first night with the minimal light of one candle and then gain in strength[59].

What is the difference between increasing light and diminishing darkness? Either way the net shift in brightness is the same. We find a similar awareness of this zero sum game in a discussion of the other rabbinic holiday, of Purim, when we are commanded[60] to drink until we don't know the difference between cursed is Haman and blessed is Mordechai[61]. In a world of binary opposites, wouldn't a blessing to Mordechai count as a curse to Haman?

King David, an ancestor of Hillel, writes in Psalms, סוּר מֵרָע וַעֲשֵׂה־טוֹב בַּקֵּשׁ שָׁלוֹם וְרָדְפֵהוּ - turn away from evil and do good, seek peace and pursue it[62]. Again, there is a connection of opposites in that the best way to remove oneself from evil is to do good. The Sefas Emes points out

---

[59] עיין הלקח והלבוב חנוכה ד' קב

[60] או"ח תרצה:א

[61] באר היטב "ארור המן בגימטריא ברוך מרדכי"

[62] תהלים לד:טו

that there are two types of fires, each correlating to different aspects of the verse[63]. There is a fire that consumes and has the capability of destroying evil and there is the illuminating light that supports doing good. He points out that humans have a fiery soul[64]. Should one start with the greatest flame to purge and torch the impurities or slowly get accustomed to being able to use and harness more and more light?

The School of Shammai sees our role in that exclusive space of pristine and intense goodness and through that great light we can minimize the negativity of the nations of the world, corresponding to the animal sacrifices on Sukkot which are correlated with the nations of the world and were offered in descending order.

Whether our initial focus should begin with the spiritual or the physical has been understood as the source of the disagreement between Jacob and Joseph in regards to which of Joseph's sons should get the blessing of the first born[65]. Ephraim comes from the plural form of the word אפר or dirt, representing the nullification of the physical[66]. Menashe has the same letters in Hebrew as the word for soul, emphasizing a spiritual focus. Joseph put Menashe first because he felt that the beginning is a focus on heaven and the soul, where Jacob corrects him and says that the proper place to start is with Ephraim and the earth, like the School of Hillel.

There is another aspect of focusing on the creation of earth that can provide guidance on how to serve God. In

---

[63] ח'א תרנ"ד

[64] כי האדם אש והיו"ד שבאיש הוא בחי' אור זרוע

[65] אמר' יוסף פ' מקץ

[66] דעת זקנים -בראשית מא:נב

TEXTUAL ACTIVISM

the story of creation, God creates everything in great multitudes. The fish, birds, and trees of the world were all created as schools, flocks, and forests. Man however, was created alone. The Talmud gives us the following reason[67]:

לפיכך נברא אדם יחידי ללמדך שכל המאבד נפש
אחת מישראל מעלה עליו הכתוב כאילו איבד עולם מלא
וכל המקיים נפש אחת מישראל מעלה עליו הכתוב כאילו
קיים עולם מלא ומפני שלום הבריות שלא יאמר אדם
לחבירו אבא גדול מאביך ושלא יהו המינים אומרים הרבה
רשויות בשמים ולהגיד גדולתו של הקב"ה שאדם טובע כמה
מטבעות בחותם אחד כולן דומין זה לזה ומלך מלכי המלכים
הקב"ה טבע כל אדם בחותמו של אדם הראשון ואין אחד
מהן דומה לחבירו לפיכך כל אחד ואחד חייב לומר בשבילי
נברא העולם

For this reason was the first human created alone: to teach that whoever destroys a single soul in Israel, Scripture sees them as though they have destroyed an entire world. And whoever saves a single soul in Israel, Scripture gives them the reward as if they had saved the entire world. Additionally, the first human was created alone for the sake of peace among people, that one shouldn't say to his/her friend, "My father was greater than yours," and so that the heretics not say that there are many governing powers in heaven. And furthermore, to declare the greatness of the Holy One, Blessed be God: in that if a person mints many coins from one mold, they all resemble one another, but when the King of Kings formed each person, in the image of Adam, and yet not one of them resembles another. Therefore, each

---

[67]סנהדרין ל"ז.

person is obligated to say: For my sake was the world created!

The greatness of God is displayed in that we are all equally created in the image of God and still we all look different. It is those differences that provide insight into the Divine, as they are a reflection of it. Like the Talmud teaches in regards to the blessing when one sees 600,000 gathered together[68].

> *הָר הרואה אוכלוסי ישראל אומר ברוך חכם הרזים שאין דעתם דומה זה לזה ואין פרצופיהן דומים זה לזה*
> When one sees multitudes of Israelites one says: 'blessed... the sage of secrets' for their minds are not similar to each other, and their faces are not similar to each other.

According to tradition, there are 600,000 letters in the Torah and Yisrael is an acronym corresponding to a head count at Mount Sinai[69]. An individual is to the nation what a letter is to the Torah. If even one is missing, it is incomplete. The Torah was never given to an individual, but to a nation. However, that nation was unified like one person with one heart[70]. It is only by including all individuals that we can receive the full Divine Revelation[71].

The parallel of the soul to a letter finds an interesting expression in a teaching of Rabbi Akiva Eiger[72].

---

[68] ברכות נח.

[69] מגלה עמוקות אופן קפו

[70] רשי שמות יט:ב

[71] כלל ישראל כאיש אחד בלב אחד = יש הרבה דרכים למקום

[72] יומא פו:

תניא היה ל"מ אומר גדולה תשובה שבשביל יחיד
שעשה תשובה מוחלין לכל העולם כולו שנא' ארפא
משובתם אוהבם נדבה כי שב אפי ממנו מהם לא נאמר אלא
ממנו

It was taught: R Meir used to say, Great is repentance. For on account of an individual who repents, the sins of all the world are forgiven, as it is said: *I will heal their backsliding. I will love them freely, for mine anger is turned away from him.* 'From them' it is not said, but 'from him.'

In his commentary in the margin he quotes from the great kabbalist Rama MiPano as understanding the passage as follows:

פירוש חלקם בברית האלה להיות ערבים זה לזה הוה הנמחל בזכותו

Meaning that each person has their "individual" soul, but also holds a part of all of the other souls.

In this context, perhaps the word "ערב", usually translated as "guarantor" might better be translated as "mixed"; All of Israel is mixed up in each other. So too with the letters of the Torah. The Sefas Emes writes about the verse תורת ה' תמימה - God's Torah is complete[73]:

פי' תמימה שבכל אות ואות נמצא כל התורה ... ולכן אין מוקדם
ומאוחר בתורה כי בכל אות יש הכל

Complete - in that each and every letter (in the Torah) is found the entire Torah... therefore there is no before or after in the Torah because each letter holds it all.

---

[73] נשא תרנ"ד

This duality of holding individual uniqueness concurrent with an awareness of the need to direct that to something greater than self is famously articulated by Hillel in the Mishnah in Tractate Avot[74]:

הוּא הָיָה אוֹמֵר, אִם אֵין אֲנִי לִי, מִי לִי. וּכְשֶׁאֲנִי לְעַצְמִי, מָה אֲנִי. וְאִם לֹא עַכְשָׁיו, אֵימָתָי.

"If am am not for myself, who will be?" highlights the obvious observation that no one else is me and therefore, I alone am responsible for being the best version of myself. However, the next phrase "And when I'm only for myself, what am I?" instructs us to realize that if I'm not part of something greater, then I'm nothing.

This might also be an allusion to another famous statement of Hillel[75]:

תניא אמרו עליו הלל הזקן כשהיה שמח בשמחת בית השואבה אמר כן אם אני כאן הכל כאן ואם איני כאן מי כאן

It was said about Hillel the elder, that when he was rejoicing at the Simchat Beit Ha'Shoeiva he said: If I am here, then everyone is here. And if I'm not here, who is here?

At face value, this arrogant statement doesn't fit with how he is portrayed by the Talmud elsewhere[76].

תּר לעולם יהא אדם ענוותן כהלל

---

[74] פרקי אבות א:יד

[75] סוכה נג.

[76] שבת ל:

It was taught: A person should always be humble like Hillel.

Rashi explains Hillel's statement:

אם אני כאן הכל כאן - דורש היה לרבים שלא יחטאו בשמו של הקב"ה אם אני כאן הכל כאן כל זמן שאני חפץ בבית הזה ושכינתי שרויה בו יהא כבודו קיים ויבאו הכל כאן ואם תחטאו ואסלק שכינתי מי יבא כאן

If I am here then all are here - He expounded publicly that people should not sin in the name of God. If I am here, all are here - As long as God wants this house and God's presence rests in it, then God's glory is sustained and everyone will come. However if one sins and the Divine presence leaves, who will come here?

The Chidushi Agadot (Rabbi Shmuel Eliezer haLevi Eidels) interprets Rashi's intention:

אם אני כאן כו'. עיין פרש"י וכינוי אני קאי על הקב"ה ושמעתי בזה עש שמספר הלל גימטרי"א אלני.

The 'I' is referring to God and I heard that the numerical value of Hillel is the same as A-donai.

Hillel sees himself and everyone else as a part, representative, and expression of God and God's holiness. We find this concept applied in the daily practice of prayer[77]. As a general principle, Proverbs[78] teaches that *in a multitude of people is a king's majesty,* so it is best to pray with a

---

[77] משנה מגילה ד:ג

[78] משלי יד:כח

large group. Yet the houses of Hillel and Shammai argue about the following situation[79]:

> תר היו יושבין בבית המדרש והביאו אור לפניהם בש״א כל אחד ואחד מברך לעצמו ובה״א אחד מברך לכולן משום שנאמר (משלי יד, כח) ברוב עם הדרת מלך בשלמא ב״ה מפרשי טעמא אלא בית שמאי מאי טעמא קסברי מפני בטול בית המדרש

> The Rabbis taught: They were sitting in the study hall and fire [for havdalah] was brought before them. Beit Shammai say that each person should make their own blessing and Beit Hillel say that one person should make the blessing for everyone because of the verse (Proverbs 14:28) 'with the multitude of the people is the glory of God'. Beit Hillel rests well as they explain their reasoning, but according to Beit Shammai, what is their reason? Because of the nullification of the study hall.

It is noteworthy that the School of Hillel offers their own reason, where it is the Talmud that provides one for the house of Shammai. Rabbi Yosef Chaim[80] suggests that the universal principle of *מצוה בו יותר מבשלוחו*[81] justifies the School of Shammai and requires the School of Hillel to offer an explanation. However, once the School of Hillel argues that in a conflict between the value of the individual and the collective, the latter wins, then the Talmud finds it necessary to explain why the School of Shammai disagrees.

---

[79] ברכות נג.

[80] בניהו שם

[81] קידושין מא.

The School of Shammai's rationale that one person's individual needs, here the need to have uninterrupted learning, will take precedence over a potentially greater communal experience is emblematic of their policies throughout the Talmud.

This valuing of individual effort is further emphasized in Bava Metzia 86b.

> אמר רב יהודה אמר רב- כל מה שעשה אברהם למלאכי השרת בעצמו עשה הקבּ״ה לבניו בעצמו וכל [מה] שעשה אברהם ע״י שליח עשה הקבּ״ה לבניו ע״י שליח.

> Everything that Abraham did himself for the angelic visitors, God then performed by God's self for the people of Israel. Everything that Abraham did through an emissary, God also does through an emissary.

If a person does an act of virtue him or herself, God resaponds by personally performing a reciprocal action. Rav Nachman Bulman z'l, shared an amazing insight on a continuation of this passage from Tractate Bava Metzia 86b:

> אמר רבי תנחום בר חנילאי- לעולם אל ישנה אדם מן המנהג שהרי משה עלה למרום ולא אכל לחם מלאכי השרת ירדו למטה ואכלו לחם ואכלו סלקא דעתך אלא אימא נראו כמי שאכלו ושתו

> A person should never deviate from the custom [of the place]. Behold, Moses went up to heaven and didn't eat bread. The angels came down here and ate. Do you think they ate? Rather say: they appeared as if they ate.

Does the Talmud intend to instruct us not to deviate from the local practice like Moses who abstains from food in Heaven; or simply not to present as deviating, like the angels who pretended to eat in Abraham's home? Rav

Bulman answered that the Talmud here is providing us with guidance for two different cases. If a person finds themselves in a place of greater holiness, then one should elevate themselves and take on the specific action in earnest. However, if a person finds themselves, as the angels did, in a less holy place, then it's important not to appear as being different. The value of the individual's action is contigent on the situation in which the individual is found. Again, the Talmud is teaching that it isn't about the action, but the direction and intention.

In this light it is clear that there isn't any competition between communal and individual Jewish practice. They both speak to making what is important to God important to us. We diminish God's glory when we try to get someone else to do an action for us. According to the School of Hillel, doing a mitzvah with others is not about saving ourselves the effort, but it is about maximizing God's glory through community.

It is noteworthy that the mitzvah to be holy was taught to the entire nation[82].

דַּבֵּר אֶל־כָּל־עֲדַת בְּנֵי־יִשְׂרָאֵל וְאָמַרְתָּ אֲלֵהֶם קְדֹשִׁים תִּהְיוּ כִּי קָדוֹשׁ אֲנִי יְקוָק אֱלֹקיכֶם:
Speak to the entire assembly of the Children of Israel and say to them: You shall be holy, for holy am I, Hashem your God.

Rashi comments:

מְלַמֵּד שֶׁנֶּאֶמְרָה פָּרָשָׁה זוּ בְּהַקְהֵל מִפְּנֵי שֶׁרוֹב גּוּפֵי תוֹרָה תְּלוּיִין בָּהּ
This teaches us that this portion was said at a gathering of the entire congregation because

---

[82] ויקרא יט:ב

the majority of the essentials of the Torah are dependant on it.

In what way is the majority of the body of Torah dependent on this *parsha*? Are there not 613 commandments, the majority of which are actually taught elsewhere? One interpretation might be that the central message of the Torah is that we should separate ourselves from our desires if those desires conflict with our relationship with God. If so, the commandment to be holy could arguably account for the majority of the Torah. The main fulfillment of the Torah and the commandments, though, is through the collective of Israel; through unity we merit holiness[83]. In other words, the concept of holiness, on which the majority of the Torah depends, is itself dependent on the unity of the Jewish People.

Shabbos is an appropriate place to demonstrate individuality in the context of unity. Shabbos is the gift of being able to cohabitate with God in an intimate space[84] [85].

אָל הקב"ה למשה מתנה טובה יש לי בבית גנזי ושבת שמה ואני מבקש ליתנה לישראל לך והודיעם
God said to Moses: I have a good gift in my treasury, and Shabbos is it's name, and I desire to give it to Israel, go and inform them.

It is interesting that Shabbos is not counted in the Talmud's list of God given gifts[86].

---

[83] שפת אמת ח'ג תרנ"ב

[84] בני ישראל את השבת ר'ת ביאה

[85] שבת י:

[86] ברכות ה.

תניא רבי שמעון בן יוחאי אומר שלש מתנות טובות נתן הקדוש ברוך הוא לישראל וכולן לא נתן אלא ע"י יסורין אלו הן תורה וארץ ישראל והעולם הבא

It was taught: Rabbi Shimon Ben Yochai said, 'There are three good gifts that God gave to Israel; and all of them were given exclusively through suffering: Torah, Israel, and the world to come.'

Perhaps, Shabbos fits under the category of the world to come, as, we are taught *שבת אחד מששים לעולם הבא*[87]. Alternatively, Shabbos can be understood as an invitation to connect and be with God, rather than an external gift that is merely received.

Shabbos is also in need of partnership, as the Midrash teaches[88]:

תָּנֵי רַבִּי שִׁמְעוֹן בֶּן יוֹחַאי, אָמְרָה שַׁבָּת לִפְנֵי הַקָּדוֹשׁ בָּרוּךְ הוּא, רִבּוֹנוֹ שֶׁל עוֹלָם לְכֻלָּן יֵשׁ בֶּן זוּג, וְלִי אֵין בֶּן זוּג. אָמַר לָהּ הַקָּדוֹשׁ בָּרוּךְ הוּא כְּנֶסֶת יִשְׂרָאֵל הִיא בֶּן זוּגֵךְ. וְכֵיוָן שֶׁעָמְדוּ יִשְׂרָאֵל לִפְנֵי הַר סִינַי אָמַר לָהֶם הַקָּדוֹשׁ בָּרוּךְ הוּא זִכְרוּ הַדָּבָר שֶׁאָמַרְתִּי לְשַׁבָּת, כְּנֶסֶת יִשְׂרָאֵל הִיא בֶּן זוּגֵךְ, הַיְנוּ דִּבּוּר (שמות כ, ח): זָכוֹר אֶת יוֹם הַשַּׁבָּת לְקַדְּשׁוֹ.

Rabbi Shimon Ben Yochai taught: Shabbos said before God 'Master of the Universe, everyone has a partner and I don't have a partner.' God said 'The Jewish People are your partner'. And when Israel stood in front of Mt. Sinai God said before them 'Remember the thing that I said to Shabbos, that Israel is the

---

[87] ברכות נז:

[88] ב"ר יא:ח

partner [of Shabbos].' This is the intent of (the verse) (Exodus 20:8) 'Remember the Shabbos to sanctify it.'

The commandment to sanctify Shabbos is expressed through the Hebrew word לקדשו which is the word that is also used for betrothal. When Israel sanctifies Shabbos, it is akin to a marriage. We find the language of holiness by Shabbos, marriage, and the relationship with the Torah because each requires a presence and expression of self to create an elevated experience.

Hillel and Shammai approached their Shabbos preparations very differently[89].

> תניא אמרו עליו על שמאי הזקן כל ימיו היה אוכל לכבוד שבת מצא בהמה נאה אומר זו לשבת מצא אחרת נאה הימנה מניח את השניה ואוכל את הראשונה אבל הלל הזקן מדה אחרת היתה לו שכל מעשיו לשם שמים שנאמר (תהלים סח, כ) ברוך ה' יום יום

> It was taught: They said about Shammai the Elder that every day he would eat in honor of the Shabbos. If he came across tasty meat, he would say 'This is for Shabbos.' If he then came across a tastier piece of meat, he would designate that one for Shabbos and then eat the first one. Hillel behaved differently, for all of his actions were for the sake of heaven, as it says: 'Blessed be God day by day.'

Shammai would spend the week saving the best delicacies for Shabbos. Hillel would enjoy the tasty things that came his way, since he had faith that God would provide him with something even better for Shabbos.

---

[89] ביצה טז.

Despite Shammai and Hillel's differing practices, the Talmud does not view this as a dispute and it is not listed by the Talmud in Shabbat 15a as one of the three matters in which they differed.

Indeed, Nachmanides points out that although the Halacha follows Hillel, Rashi quotes Shammai's interpretation in his commentary on Exodus 20:8[90].

זָכוֹר אֶת־יוֹם הַשַּׁבָּת לְקַדְּשׁוֹ וְכֵן פִּתְרוֹנוֹ: תְּנוּ לֵב לִזְכּוֹר תָּמִיד אֶת יוֹם הַשַּׁבָּת, שֶׁאִם נִזְדַּמֵּן לְךָ חֵפֶץ יָפֶה תְּהֵא מַזְמִינוֹ לַשַּׁבָּת (מכילתא):

> A person should constantly align their heart to remember the Shabbos; that if one should come across something nice to eat, they should save it for Shabbos.

The Bayit Chadash understands that the Talmud, and Hillel himself, hold Shammai's position to be preferable, but it is up to people to choose the approach that best fits with their spiritual practice. He writes:

> אמרו עליו על שמאי הזקן וכו' משמע דלא פליגי אלא שזה
> כך היה מדתו וזה כך היה מדתו וביד כל אדם לאחוז במנהג
> שמאי הזקן או במנהג הלל הזקן... מצאתי שכתב אף על גב
> דמדה אחרת היתה בהלל הזקן אלא מודה הלל דמדת שמאי
> עדיפא טפי וכן משמע במעשה דההוא קצב בפ' כל כתבי
> שאמר וכל בהמה נאה שמצאתי אמרתי זו לכבוד שבת וכו'
> והכי עיקר:

---

[90] The Bi'ur B'Sadeh writes; "Everyone agrees that we need to remember the Shabbos constantly, in whichever way that we can, like we mention the days of the week in relation to Shabbos." The Sifsei Chachamim understands Rashi's intent as limiting the verse to thoughts of remembering. He supports the claim that if the word *zachor* was meant to command an action, there wouldn't be a *kamatz* under the *zayin*.

The Talmud's choice of the word "*מדה*", meaning a character trait, implies a reflection of Shammai the person, not a legal approach.

This supports the premise that it's not about the action being performed, but rather, that the manifestation is a result of an authentic expression of self in divine service. Shammai celebrated Shabbos as he did because of the kind of person that he was[91].

> *והאר חנינא משום ר' שמעון בן יוחי אין לו להקב״ה בבית גנזיו אלא אוצר של יראת שמים שנאמר (ישעיהו לג, ו) יראת ה' היא אוצרו.*

Rabbi Chanina said, in the name of Rabbi Shimon Bar Yochai, 'God only has the fear of heaven in God's storehouse, as it says: *Fear of God is in His storehouse.*'

Shammai approaches his service of God from a place of awe and fear. This allow him to be punctilious, but also not always pleasant. Indeed, the Talmud warns us not to emulate Shammai's personality[92] - *ואל יהא קפדן כשמאי* - Do not be overly particular, like Shammai.

We find in the narrative of the Talmud three accounts of gentiles who approached both Shammai and Hillel to convert[93]:

> *ת״ר מעשה בנכרי אחד שבא לפני שמאי אמר לו כמה תורות יש לכם אמר לו שתים תורה שבכתב ותורה שבעל פה אל*

---

[91] ברכות לג:

[92] שבת ל:

[93] שבת לא.

שבכתב אני מאמינך ושבעל פה איני מאמינך גייריה עִם
שתלמדני תורה שבכתב גער בו והוציאו בנזיפה בא לפני
הלל גייריה יומא קמא א״ל א״ב ג״ד למחר אפיך ליה א״ל והא
אתמול לא אמרת לי הכי א״ל לאו עלי דידי קא סמכת דעל
פה נמי סמוך עלי:
שוב מעשה בנכרי אחד שבא לפני שמאי א״ל גיירני עִם
שתלמדני כל התורה כולה כשאני עומד על רגל אחת דחפו
באמת הבנין שבידו בא לפני הלל גייריה אמר לו דעלך סני
לחברך לא תעביד זו היא כל התורה כולה ואידך פירושה
הוא זיל גמור.
שוב מעשה בנכרי אחד שהיה עובר אחורי בית המדרש
ושמע קול סופר שהיה אומר (שמות כח, ד) ואלה הבגדים
אשר יעשו חושן ואפוד אמר הללו למי אמרו לו לכהן גדול
אמר אותו נכרי בעצמו אלך ואתגייר בשביל שישימוני כהן
גדול בא לפני שמאי אמר ליה גיירני על מנת שתשימני כהן
גדול דחפו באמת הבנין שבידו בא לפני הלל גייריה.
אל כלום מעמידין מלך אלא מי שיודע טכסיסי מלכות לך
למוד טכסיסי מלכות הלך וקרא כיון שהגיע (במדבר א, נא)
והזר הקרב יומת אמר ליה מקרא זה על מי נאמר א״ל אפי'
על דוד מלך ישראל נשא אותו גר קל וחומר בעצמו ומה
ישראל שנקראו בנים למקום ומתוך אהבה שאהבם קרא
להם (שמות ד, כב) בני בכורי ישראל כתיב עליהם והזר
הקרב יומת גר הקל שבא במקלו ובתרמילו על אחת כמה
וכמה.
בא לפני שמאי א״ל כלום ראוי אני להיות כהן גדול והלא
כתיב בתורה והזר הקרב יומת בא לפני הלל א״ל ענוותן הלל
ינוחו לך ברכות על ראשך שהקרבתני תחת כנפי השכינה
לימים נזדווגו שלשתן למקום אחד אמרו קפדנותו של שמאי
בקשה לטורדנו מן העולם ענוותנותו של הלל קרבנו תחת
כנפי השכינה.

Our Rabbis taught: A certain heathen once came before Shammai and asked him, 'How many Torahs have you?' 'Two,' he replied: 'the Written Torah and the Oral Torah.' 'I believe you with respect to the Written, but not with respect to the Oral Torah; make me a proselyte on condition that you teach me the Written Torah.' He scolded and repulsed him in anger. When he went before Hillel, he accepted him as a proselyte. On the first day, he taught him, Alef, Beth, Gimmel, Daled. The following day he reversed [them] to him. 'But yesterday you did not teach them to me like this,' he protested. 'Must you then not rely upon me? Then rely upon me with respect to the Oral [Torah] too.'

On another occasion it happened that a certain heathen came before Shammai and said to him, 'Make me a proselyte, on condition that you teach me the whole Torah while I stand on one foot.' Thereupon he repulsed him with the builder's cubit which was in his hand. When he went before Hillel, he said to him, 'What is hateful to you, do not to your neighbor, that is the whole Torah while the rest is commentary thereof; go and learn it.'

On another occasion it happened that a certain heathen was passing behind a Beit Ha'Midrash, when he heard the voice of a teacher reciting, 'And these are the garments which they shall make; a breastplate, and an ephod.' He said, 'For whom are these?' 'For the High Priest,' he was told. Then said that heathen to himself, 'I will go and become a proselyte, that I may be appointed a High Priest.' So he went before Shammai and said to him, 'Make me a proselyte on condition that you appoint me a High Priest.' But he repulsed him with the builder's cubit which was in his hand. He then went before Hillel, who made him a proselyte. He said 'Can any man be made a king but he who knows the arts of government? Go and study the arts of government!' He went and read. When he came to the verse, *and the stranger that comes shall be put to death,* he asked Hillel, 'To whom does this verse apply?' 'Even to David King, of Israel,' was the answer. Thereupon that proselyte reasoned within himself a fortiori: if Israel, who are called sons of the Omnipresent, and who in His love for them He designated them, *Israel is my son, my firstborn,* yet it is written of them, *and the stranger that comes shall be put to death* how much more so a mere proselyte, who comes with his staff and wallet! Then he went before Shammai and said to him, 'Am I then eligible to be a High Priest; is it not written in the Torah, *and the stranger that comes shall be put to death*?' He went before Hillel and said to him, 'Gentle Hillel; blessings rest on your head for bringing me under the wings of the Shechinah!' Some time later the three met in one place; said they, 'Shammai's impatience sought to drive us from the world, but Hillel's gentleness brought us under the wings of the Divine Presence.'

These accounts are helpful in providing more insight into how Hillel and Shammai react to an outsider who wants to be part of the Jewish people. When Hillel distills the entire Torah to "a commentary on what your friend doesn't like, don't do. Now go and learn," he recontextualizes Judaism as a relationship with God where the Torah contains the details of that relationship. Rashi explains the "friend" as being God:

ריעך . . . זה הקב"ה על תעבור על דבריו שהרי עליך
שנאוי שיעבור חבירך על דבריך

Friend...this is God; don't transgress God's words for you wouldn't like it if your friend didn't follow your wishes.

Hillel comes from a place of love and compassion.

He tries to advance growth and understanding and he recognizes that other perspectives can and should have space as well.

Shammai is worried about getting it wrong and is willing to have less growth in order to operate safely. Shammai is so anxious about mistakes that his students argue about whether it would have been preferable to never have been born[94]:

> תר שתי שנים ומחצה נחלקו ב״ש וב״ה הללו אומרים נוח לו
> לאדם שלא נברא יותר משנברא והללו אומרים נוח לו
> לאדם שנברא יותר משלא נברא נמנו וגמרו נוח לו לאדם
> שלא נברא יותר משנברא עכשיו שנברא יפשפש במעשיו
> ואמרי לה ימשמש במעשיו
>
> For two and a half years Beit Shammai and Beit Hillel argued: 'Better that humanity should never have been created.' And they would say: 'Better that humanity was created moreso than if not'. They counted and ultimately concluded that it would have been better that we not have been created, but now that we are here, we should examine our actions.

Focusing on being more elitist and exclusive allowed the School of Shammai to have a higher caliber of students, although they were fewer in number[95].

> תר אבא אמר שמואל שלש שנים נחלקו ב״ש וב״ה הללו
> אומרים הלכה כמותנו והללו אומרים הלכה כמותנו יצאה
> בת קול ואמרה אלו ואלו דברי אלהים חיים הן והלכה כב״ה
> וכי מאחר שאלו ואלו דברי אלהים חיים מפני מה זכו ב״ה

---

[94] עירובין יג:

[95] יבמות יד.

> לקבוע הלכה כמותן מפני שנוחין ועלובין היו ושונין דבריהן
> ודברי ב"ש ולא עוד אלא שמקדימין דברי ב"ש לדבריהן
>
> Rabbi Abba stated in the name of Samuel: For three years there was a dispute between Beit Shammai and Beit Hillel. These said, the law is like us and these said, the law is like us. A voice from Heaven announced, these and those are the words of the living God and the law is like Beit Hillel. After we have established that both these and those are the words of a living God, why did Hillel merit to have the law follow their position? Because they were pleasant and agreeable and they taught the words of Beit Shammai along with their own, and even taught the words of Beit Shammai before (teaching) their own words.[96]

It seems that this aspect of humility is what tilted the scales in heaven that the law follows the School of Hillel.

Hillel, in the mystical tradition balances out Shammai. Adonai is *midas harachamim* (the trait of mercy), which has the same numerical value as Hillel[97],[98].

> הֲדָא הוּא דִכְתִיב (משלי יא, יז): גֹּמֵל נַפְשׁוֹ אִישׁ חָסֶד, זֶה הִלֵּל הַזָּקֵן,
>
> So it is written (Proverbs 11:17): 'A man of kindness brings good upon himself'; this is Hillel the Elder.

---

[96] עירובין יג:

[97] זהר ח'א ד'לא ע"א

[98] ו'ר לד:ג

Hillel was able to connect the day to the night and to bring more compassion into this world[99]. Hillel pursued peace even at expense of truth, and saw the *lo lishma* aspects of the human experience as necessary to achieve the higher levels of truth[100].

Hillel and Shammai are understood as reincarnations of Abel, as is Moses. Hillel comes from the side of *chesed* and Shammai from the side of *gevurah*. Shammai sinned by having too much *gevurah*. He is reincarnated as Shimon ben Azzai, who doesn't marry. Like Abraham, Shimon ben Azzai creates souls by dedicating his life to Torah, and to the need of the Torah to be complete with people.

Unlikely mixtures are sometimes referred to as *l'shem shamayim*. The Midrash explains the phrase *l'shem shamayim* as a blend of fire and water, both literally and figuratively. It is interesting that we are taught that the word "good" is missing from the creation story on the day that the waters were separated and the heavens were created. This could be because on that day division and separation were created. The commentaries push back and point out that on the first day there was also the separation between light and dark. The difference is that water naturally binds and comes together, darkness is just the absence of light.

The Seforno speaks to the value added worth of the unity of creation by pointing out the narrative change in wording from "good" to "very good." When things exist by themselves they can be good, but when they come together for a greater cause than self, it becomes very good. It is interesting to note that the word *shamayim* (heaven) appears 100 times in the Torah. The word *shem*

---

[99] פרי הארץ ח'ד ד'פג

[100] תלדות יעקב יוסף ח'ג ד'תמה

(name) appears 100 times in Psalms[101]. This suggests that the goal in all of our actions is the reunification of the Torah and people.

Even though there were disagreements in practice, there was still a way in which people were able to get along[102].

אעפ שאלו אוסרים ואלו מתירין אלו פוסלין ואלו מכשירין לא נמנעו בית שמאי מלישא נשים מבית הלל ולא בית הלל מבית שמאי כל הטהרות והטמאות שהיו אלו מטהרים ואלו מטמאין לא נמנעו עושין טהרות אלו על גבי אלו

Even though these prohibited and these permitted, these invalidated and these deemed fit, still Beit Shammai didn't refrain from marrying women from Beit Hillel nor did Beit Hillel (refrain) from (marrying women from) Beit Shammai. All of the produce, pure and impure, that these would deem pure and these would deem impure, they didn't hold back from handling for the other.

There is a way in which we are more complicated than God. The Ramchal writes in Derech Hashem that we have different aspects of ourselves compartmentalized in separate spaces. Memory is different than touch which is separate from taste. God, however holds all things simultaneously in complete unity without any parts. God is one.

We, unlike God, occupy a physical and finite space. By definition, we need to have a finite commitment to that space. But in truth, this is only that way superficially.

---

[101] מגלה עמוקות פ'לך

[102] יבמות יג:

Below the surface we are able to see and hold all of those contradictory and mutually exclusive aspects simultaneously.

I think that the greatest expression of this idea in Jewish ritual practice comes on the first night of Passover. Understanding the hidden nature of things requires practice and sensitivity training. The Talmud teaches us that thirty days before Passover we are meant to start preparing.

The Shulchan Aruch teaches that we are able to establish the Hebrew calendar from the first night of Passover. The mnemonic for this is an את ב״ש where the days of the week correspond to the festivals. If the first day of Passover is Monday, then the ninth of Av will also be on a Monday. This continues for all of the festivals until the sixth night, that correlates to Purim. Instead of predicting the date of Purim in the coming year, it reflects back on the date of the previous Purim, the one from a month ago. This affirms Purim as a preparatory act for Passover.

On Purim, we focus on seeing that which is hidden. The holiday celebrates a hidden miracle. Esther comes from a word meaning hidden. God's name does not appear anywhere in the Megillah. The custom is to wear masks that hide our identity. We eat hamantaschen, in which the filling is concealed until it's often too late. As the wine goes in, the hidden secrets come out.

If there is one holiday that represents the unity, love, and togetherness of the Jewish people, it is Purim. The Talmud in Shabbos teaches that at the time of Purim we accepted the Torah again, but this time out of love. We had the same unity that was achieved by the giving of the Torah at Sinai, but this time there was no religious coercion.

It is noteworthy that Purim is the only holiday in the Jewish calendar that can't be celebrated by all of the Jewish people in unison on the same day, because it has a different day for those living in walled cities. Unity isn't everyone doing the same thing in the same way. It is specifically when the space is given for creative expression of that which isn't limited by the external. We are able to balance the reality that one person's Purim *seudah* / meal will look different than another's, but we can share something of ours and incorporate some of theirs.

It is perhaps in this way that we are able to understand the Zohar that teaches that Yom Kippur is a *Yom K'Purim*. A day like Purim. On Yom Kippur, we are worried about our own souls and sins. On Purim we care about the needs of others, seeing the spiritual in the physical, while embracing the physical, not denying it.

This prepares us for the night of Passover. Every aspect of Passover holds contradicting meanings. The matzah is both the poor person's bread of affliction, and the bread of Israelite freedom. The wine, an intoxicating luxurious libation is ideally meant to be red to remind us of the blood. The bitter herbs are green for rebirth and life. Charoset is sweet, but represents the mortar. The act of dipping represents freedom, but we dip in saltwater to remind us of the tears that were shed.

The night shifts into day. We see things with clarity. It is the only biblical mitzvah that can be performed exclusively at night. There is no fear of the evil inclination. In the song at the end of the haggadah, we occupy a space in a futuristic time when the angel of death has already been slaughtered.

The masculine shifts to the feminine. There are four cups of wine, sons, languages of redemption, and questions. But four is the number of our matriarchs. We bless the feminine omnipresent, celebrate the birth of a nation, and move through a narrow constricted place into vast expansiveness. The fifteen stages of the haggadah mirror the cycle that reflects the moon and both the physical and spiritual assents of the steps and songs of the temple.

We focus on the quality of those who say more as praiseworthy. Speech is the process of taking hidden thoughts, feelings, and ideas and bringing them to revelation. Passover is Pesach פה סח the mouth that speaks. The mitzvah of telling the story, eating matzah, drinking wine all involve the mouth. Pharaoh, comes from a language of evil mouth. The matzah is the thing that we say a lot about.

Moses is left out of our retelling of the Passover story at the Seder. The Maharal explains his speech impediment as his inability to verbalize what he saw when he experienced God, because words are limited and couldn't possibly express his experience. Perhaps that is why it would be inappropriate for him to be part of the telling over of the story.

Our rabbis tell us that the Torah can be understood on four basic levels. The simple (פשט), the homiletic (דרש), through allusions (רמז), and in the mystical plane (סוד). In Hebrew, the first letter of these four levels spells the word for orchard. On the night of Passover, nothing is simple, no פשט. The matzah is not about flour and water. When we remove the letter associated with the simple (פשט), we are left with: סדר- *seder* (order). Authentic order and truth is when we look above and below the limited superficial to uncover and reunify the depths of the eternal and infinite.

זֵכֶר לְמִקְדָּשׁ כְּהִלֵּל. כֵּן עָשָׂה הִלֵּל בִּזְמַן שֶׁבֵּית הַמִּקְדָּשׁ הָיָה קַיָּם: הָיָה כּוֹרֵךְ פסח מַצָּה וּמָרוֹר וְאוֹכֵל בְּיַחַד, לְקַיֵּם מַה שֶּׁנֶּאֱמַר: עַל מַצּוֹת וּמְרוֹרִים יֹאכְלֻהוּ.

As a remembrance to the Temple like Hillel. This is what Hillel did while the Temple was standing: He would wrap the paschal lamb in matzah with bitter herbs and eat it together as a way of fulfilling the verse *with matzah and bitters herbs you shall eat them.*

The Talmud teaches that the second Temple was destroyed because of baseless hatred. It is interesting that for the destruction of the first temple, which we are told was due to the three cardinal sins, we received seventy years of exile, but for not being nice we are still homeless 2000 years later! R' Matisyahu Salomon, Mashgiach of Beth Medrash Govoha explains that it isn't a punishment, it is just the reality. If we can't get along as siblings, than we can't be with God as our parent.

One of the first declarations of the night is "anyone who is hungry let them come and eat." The focus of the night is communal responsibility. We answer the four sons because of the need to make sure that they understand, not because I have a need to teach. The paschal sacrifice is a communal one. We were united then as a nation, but each one of us has the obligation to tell our own story.

It is rather remarkable that we are meant to remember the Temple, because it is no longer standing, the way that Hillel "remembered it" while it was still standing. Hillel's profound understanding of the need of the collective allowed him to appreciate it, and more importantly, to demonstrate it. We should remember the temple the way that Hillel did, bending in order to combine everything together so that it can come together in the ultimate sweetness of true Godliness.

On the Seder night, and indeed on all nights, we must remember the importance of coming together as a community and especially of welcoming in folks who are on the margins. God contains all within God's self and we can only be a community of God if everyone can find their place in our community.

BALANCING SOLO AND COMMUNAL JEWISH PRACTICE

In the world of social justice, showing up for a cause is a core value. Individual action and personal participation is prioritized. This emphasis on each person's contribution is analogous to the Talmud's concept of "*מצוה בו יותר מבשלוחו*" - "it is a better mitzvah to do it yourself than through a representative." Yet the Talmud also has a contravening principle[103] "*ברב עם הדרת מלך*" "with the multitudes of the people is the glory of God" – which is understood as valuing a large mass of people selecting one representative to act on their behalf. This essay seeks to explore these two competing modalities and to create a framework for discerning when it is better to act as part of a collective and when it is better to stand on one's own.

Certain mitzvot privilege individual performance while others are best fulfilled communally. For example, the law regarding the reading of the Megillah is that although one may read it alone, it is still better for it to be read in a large group[104]. By contrast, when searching for chametz, the Halacha is that although one may search a house on behalf of all those who live there, each person should still be involved in the search because of "*מצוה בו יותר מבשלוחו*"[105].

---

[103] משלי יד:כח

[104] ערוך השלחן או"ח תרפז:ה

[105] משנה ברורה תלב:ח

The tension between these competing principles is at the core of the Tannaitic dispute concerning how to perform the Saturday night ritual of havdalah[106].

תָּנוּ רָבָּנָן הָיוּ יוֹשְׁבִין בְּבֵית הַמִּדְרָשׁ וְהֵבִיאוּ אוֹר לִפְנֵיהֶם בש"א כל אחד ואחד מברך לעצמו ובה"א אחד מברך לכולן משום שנאמר (משלי יד, כח) בְּרָב עָם הַדְרַת מֶלֶךְ בשלמא ב"ה מפרשי טעמא אלא בית שמאי מאי טעמא קסברי מפני בטול בית המדרש:

We learn in a Baraita[107]: "If people were sitting in the study hall and light was brought before them, Beit Shammai say 'Each one makes the blessing for themselves.' Beit Hillel say: 'One should say the blessing for everyone. Because it is stated: *With the multitude of people is the glory of the King.*'" It rests well with Beit Hillel, for they explain their reason, but Beit Shammai, what is their reasoning? They hold because of the nullification of the study hall.

Rabbi Yosef Chaim[108] observes the structural asymmetry in the Baraita that only Beit Hillel brings a proof text to support their position[109], but Beit Shammai's reasoning isn't given. He further understands the question

---

[106] ברכות נג.

[107] תוספתא פ"ה ע"ש

[108] ספר בניהו שם

[109] It is interesting that the Tosefta teaches this dispute without any reasoning given and the positions are reversed:
בית המדרש ב"ש אומרים אחד מברך לכולן וב"ה אומרי' כל אחד ואח' מברך עצמו.
Additionally, the *Mesoret Ha-Shas* cites the source of this Baraita to be the Tosefta in the fifth chapter of Berachot. If this is true, then the *stama* of the gemara brings the *Bi-Shelama* before the first verse.

of the *stama* of the gemara not to be about Beit Shammai's underlying reason, but rather a response to Beit Hillel's reasoning. He posits that originally Beit Shammai relied on the principle of "מצוה בו יותר מבשלוחו", it is better to do a mitzvah yourself than through an emissary. It is to that reasoning that Beit Hillel respond with the verse, arguing that it is stronger than the original principle. The Talmud, curious how Beit Shammai might defend his position, offers the argument that although "ברוב עם הדרת מלך", that principle would not obtain in a situation where it would result in the nullification of Torah study. Perhaps the *Stama* engages in the pursuit of understanding Beit Shammai, even though the Halacha doesn't follow them, in order to better understand the working parts and motivations of Beit Hillel, to be able to apply them more globally around conflicts of solo and communal Jewish practice.

It is no accident that the discussion of individual and communal performance of havdalah involves a candle. The verse teaches[110] - נֵר יְהוָה נִשְׁמַת אָדָם חֹפֵשׂ כָּל־חַדְרֵי־בָטֶן: "The soul of a person, is the candle of God, which searches the chambers of one's innards." The candle symbolizes a person's soul and the reader is invited to ask, "When should my candle be part of a multi-wicked one, and when should it stand alone in the darkness of the exile? How do I know what God wants my candle to be?" Perhaps this is the internal searching of which the verse speaks, in that what we do with our individual light shows our most inner motivations.

If Judaism is the relationship that God intends to have with the Jewish people, then the Torah contains the details of that relationship. The Torah is also compared to

---

[110] משלי כ:כז

a candle, like Rashi interprets the verse[111]:

> נֵר־לְרַגְלִי דְבָרֶךָ וְאוֹר לִנְתִיבָתִי
> Your word is a lamp for my feet and a light for my path.

Rashi writes:

> כשאני בא להורות הוראה אני רואה בתורה והיא מפרשת אותי מן האסור כנר המציל את האד' מן הפחתים
> When I come to answer a question in Jewish law, I look into the Torah and she seperates me from that which is prohibited like a candle saves a person from obstacles.

We find the Tannaitic source for "מצוה בו יותר מבשלוחו" in the beginning of the second chapter of Kiddushin:

> הָאִישׁ מְקַדֵּשׁ בּוֹ וּבִשְׁלוּחוֹ. הָאִשָּׁה מִתְקַדֶּשֶׁת בָּהּ וּבִשְׁלוּחָהּ. הָאִישׁ מְקַדֵּשׁ אֶת בִּתּוֹ כְּשֶׁהִיא נַעֲרָה, בּוֹ וּבִשְׁלוּחוֹ.
> A man can betroth personally, or through his agent. A woman can become betrothed personally, or through her agent. A man may give his daughter in betrothal when she is a *na'arah*, personally or through his agent.

We learn about the importance of individual action from the laws of marriage. The Mishnah teaches that although we can effect a betrothal through an agent, it is better to become betrothed in person. It is the most intimate and exclusive of relationships, marriage, that is chosen by the Mishnah to be the starting point of our relationship with God when we are encouraged to show

---

[111] תהלים קיט:קה

up as an individual and be present[112]. It is noteworthy, that although *shlichut* (agency) is a principle throughout the Torah, and mentioned in other mishnayot, it is specifically here, in discussing marriage, where the *sugya* (topic) is primarily developed. This is especially notheworthy as the Talmud here learns the source from a verse about divorce and then applies it to marriage through a *heikesh* (Talmudic hermeneutical exegesis). Yet even though tractate Gittin (which deals with divorce) appears earlier in the order of the mishnayot, and the source for the *heikish* is learnt from there, why did the sages primarily develop the topic here rather than earlier?

The Acharonim put forth an understanding that there are two separate laws being taught in our mishnah. One is the ability to affect the application of the representation and the second is the ability to fulfill the action. This will be explained soon. A simpler explanation might be that divorce is not a mitzvah, even on the man, the same way that getting married is, and therefore Rebbe, in redacting the Mishnah, chose to teach it specifically here[113].

---

[112] The ק מרוז'ין זיע'א ס"writes: the man referred to in the mishnah is God, like the Gemara in Sotah 42b "there is no man except God" as it says in Exodus 15:13, "God, man of war." He understands the mishnah to be teaching that there are two ways for God to save the Jewish people (homiletically through the intimacy of marriage between God and the Jewish people). We can be redeemed through God, Godself, or through an emissary. When the Gemara says "השתא בשלוחו מקדש"
what it means is that until now, we the Jewish people have found freedom to be close through the many messengers of God, but now:
"בו מבעיא!"
we want God, Godself, to be the one to bring redemption.

[113] עיין בעטרת שמואל

We find this replicated by Maimonides in Mishneh Torah. In regards to marriage he writes[114]:

יֵשׁ לָאִישׁ לַעֲשׂוֹת שָׁלִיחַ לְקַדֵּשׁ לוֹ אִשָּׁה בֵּין אִשָּׁה בֵּין פְּלוֹנִית בֵּין אִשָּׁה מִשְׁאָר הַנָּשִׁים.

There is (the ability) for a man to make a representative, שָׁלִיחַ, to marry a woman for him...

However, in the laws of divorce he doesn't deploy the word "שָׁלִיחַ" at all[115].

זֶה שֶׁנֶּאֱמַר בַּתּוֹרָה (דברים כד א)"וְכָתַב לָהּ סֵפֶר כְּרִיתֻת וְנָתַן בְּיָדָהּ. אֶחָד הַכּוֹתֵב בְּיָדוֹ אוֹ שֶׁאָמַר לְאַחֵר לִכְתֹּב לוֹ. וְאֶחָד הַנּוֹתֵן בְּיָדוֹ אוֹ שֶׁאָמַר לְאַחֵר לִתֵּן לָהּ.

This that it says in the Torah: "And you will write a document of divorce and give it in her hand." One may write it or may have another write it. One may give it himself or may tell another to give it to her.

One approach that is offered by Rabbi Chaim Soloveitchik[116] is that marriage is a special type of acquisition, more specific than just representing someone's interests because of the verse[117] "כִּי־יִקַּח אִישׁ אִשָּׁה וּבָא אֵלֶיהָ וּשְׂנֵאָהּ", specifically "when you take."

The Babylonian Talmud is bothered why it is necessary to teach both that a person can get married by

---

[114] אישות ג:ד

[115] גירושין ב:א

[116] ברכת שמואל ס' י

[117] דברים כב:יג

themselves and through a representative. If it works through a representative, obviously it works through the person themselves! This is the first question of the Gemara in the chapter:

השתא בשלוחו מקדש בו מיבעיא

In the process of asking this question, the word "*בו*" is highlighted. Upon a closer reading it would appear that the Mishnah should have written: "*האיש מקדש הוא ושלוחו*." The word "*בו*" seems odd. So why is "*בו*" necessary?

The Gemara answers, quoting Rav Yosef: *אמר רב יוסף מצוה בו יותר מבשלוחו*. The intention of the Tanna of our mishnah was to teach the principle of *מצוה בו יותר מבשלוחו*.

In which case there is no redundancy because the Mishnah is teaching two separate ideas: firstly, that *shlichut* (agency) works for marriage, and secondly that it is in someway deficient to do it that way.

Although "*מצוה בו יותר מבשלוחו*" doesn't appear in the Jerusalem Talmud, I don't see this gemara, in the Bavli, as an example of the scriptilization of the Mishnah. The bulkiness of the language invites the reader to ask what is being concealed. The Jerusalem Talmud can be read with the same intention. The question in the Yerushalmi is implied and the resolution is, by contrast, in opposition. Why did the Mishnah find it necessary to teach both cases? In order to equate them to each other.

The Gemara doesn't ask "How do we know that *shlichut* (agency) works?," but "How do we know that the *shaliach* (agent) is equal and like the principal themself?"

מניין ששלוחו של אדם כמותו אמר רבי לעזר (שמות יב) ושחטו אותו כל קהל עדת ישראל בין הערבים וכי כולן שוחטין אותו והלא אחד הוא שהוא שוחט על ידי כולם אלא מיכן ששלוחו של אדם כמותו

From where do we know that the emissary is like the person himself? Rebbi Luzar says (from the verse) "the entire congregation of the assembly of Israel shall slaughter it in the afternoon." And is everyone slaughtering it?! Does one not slaughter on behalf of everyone? From here you see that the representative is like the person themselves.

It is not clear from the text of the Babylonian Talmud, explicitly, in what way it is better to do the mitzvah yourself. Rashi explains[118]:

מצוה בו יותר מבשלוחו - דכי עסיק גופו במצות מקבל שכר טפי:
When a person involves their own body in a mitzvah, they receive more reward.

It would seem that the word "בו", in the mishnah, is both referring to the body of a person and the concept taught, but clearly not innovated, by Rav Yosef[119].

How are we meant to understand this principle? Is it a broad external concept that applies globally to divine service or is it an integral component to every mitzvah? If I create a more difficult environment, say standing on one foot while putting on Tefillin, do I earn more reward? Does it extend to going to the store to buy tzitzit myself, as opposed to having them delivered to my door? Or, if I have be asked to perform a mitzvah on behalf of group of people and then someone more important becomes

---

[118] Rashi, understood simply, is teaching that יַשְׁכִּים בַּבֹּקֶר is not an obligation, but a better version. We find a similar understanding in

יַשְׁכִּים בַּבֹּקֶר בַּיּוֹם הַשִּׁשִּׁי לְהָכִין צָרְכֵי שַׁבָּת, וַאֲפִלּוּ יֵשׁ לוֹ כַּמָּה עֲבָדִים לְשַׁמְּשׁוֹ יִשְׁתַּדֵּל לְהָכִין בְּעַצְמוֹ שׁוּם דָּבָר לְצָרְכֵי שַׁבָּת כְּדֵי לְכַבְּדוֹ, כִּי רַב חִסְדָּא הָיָה מְחַתֵּךְ הַיָּרָק דַּק דַּק; שו"ע או"ח סי רנ:א

[119] שיעור' רב' אליהו ברוך

available to do the mitzvah, am I allowed to let them take my place[120]?

To try and answer these questions it would be helpful to first explore to what mitzvah is the Mishnah referring. The Talmud brings a support for this tradition from Rav Safra and Rava:

כי הא דרב ספרא מחריך רישא רבא מלח שיבוטא

It is interesting to note that this statement is part of a larger list brought in a conversation about doing things for the Shabbos in the gemara in Shabbos[121].

רב ספרא מחריך רישא רבא מלח שיבוטא רב הונא מדליק שרגי רב פפא גדיל פתילתא רב חסדא פרים סילקא רבה ורב יוסף מצלחי ציבי ר' זירא מצתת צתותי

Rav Safra would singe the head. Rava would salt the fish. Rav Huna would light lamps. Rav Pappa would twine the wicks. Rav Chisda would mince the beets. Rabbah and Rav Yosef would split wood. R' Zeira would kindle fire.

Rav Yosef is a third generation Amora in Bavel. Although Rav Safra and Rava lived later, Rav Huna and Rav Chisda are a generation earlier. Clearly the tradition and custom predated Rav Yosef and were just recorded in his name.

What were the Rabbis fulfilling with these actions? How were they permitted to stop learning Torah in order to engage in these acts that could have been done by others? This is a *מצוה שאפשר לעשותה ע"י אחרים* and it is

---

[120] כתב המגן אברהם רנ:ב "וה"ה בכל מצוה, מצוה בו יותר מבשלוחו

[121] שבת קיט:

forbidden to stop learning Torah to do a mitzvah that someone else can do[122]. How does this level of obligation parallel the level of mitzvah in our mishnah?

Maimonides writes in the laws of Shabbos[123]:

אַרְבָּעָה דְבָרִים נֶאֶמְרוּ בְּשַׁבָּת. שְׁנַיִם מִן הַתּוֹרָה. וּשְׁנַיִם מִדִּבְרֵי סוֹפְרִים וְהֵן מְפֹרָשִׁין עַל יְדֵי הַנְּבִיאִים. שֶׁבַּתּוֹרָה (שמות כ ז)"זָכוֹר" ְ (דברים ה יא)"שָׁמוֹר". וְשֶׁנִּתְפָּרְשׁוּ עַל יְדֵי הַנְּבִיאִים כָּבוֹד וָעֹנֶג שֶׁנֶּאֱמַר (ישעיה נח יג)"וְקָרָאתָ לַשַּׁבָּת עֹנֶג וְלִקְדוֹשׁ ה' מְכֻבָּד":

Four things were said about Shabbos. Two are from the Torah and two are from the words of the Rabbis and are explained through the Prophets. From the Torah, "Remember" (*zachor*) and "Guard" (*shamor*). And explained through the Prophets "Honor" (*kavod*) and "Delight" (*oneg*) as the verse in Isaiah says: *If you call the Shabbos "delight," the Lord's day "honored."*

The Vilna Gaon explains this Rambam to distinguish *oneg* from *kavod* to be determined by when the action is happening. He writes that *oneg* is on Shabbos itself, whereas *kavod* is on the eve of Shabbos[124]. These Rabbis were engaged in these activities for Shabbos before Shabbos started. Were they fulfilling the actual mitzvah of honoring the shabbat or were they just enabling the fulfillment of the mitzvah of *oneg* later on?

These stories are coming out of the teaching of our mishnah, which is helpful in that we can examine the mitzvah level of marriage in the mishnah to shed light on

---

[122] שלחן ערוך הרב רנ:ב

[123] ל:א

[124] ביאור הגר"א או"ח תקכט:א

these acts for Shabbos. It also seems that the Talmud is reinforcing the model of relationship by framing this conversation around Shabbos[125]. Additionally, there is a comparison brought between the distance between us and God during the week as analogous to a mitzvah done through an emissary[126], whereas Shabbos is analogous to a direct and intimate service[127].

How does the mitzvah of Shabbos correlate to the mitzvah of marriage? The Ran writes:

ואע"ג דאשה אינה מצווה בפריה ורביה מ"מ יש לה מצוה מפני שהיא מסייעת לבעל לקיים מצותו.

And even though a woman isn't obligated in the mitzvah of procreation, nevertheless she has a mitzvah because she assists her husband in fulfilling his mitzvah.

It would appear, according to the Ran, that marriage for the man isn't an obligation by itself, but only the means by which to fulfill his real obligation of having children. This is also the position of the Rosh, in Kesubos[128], who writes that the blessings over getting married are not considered blessings over a mitzvah, but rather blessings of praise. He explains that getting married is only considered a *הכשר מצוה*.

Maimonides, by contrast, understands marriage to be

---

[125] תני ר"ש בן יוחאי: אמרה שבת לפני הקב"ה "רבש"ע לכולן יש בן זוג, ולי אין בן זוג", א"ל הקב"ה "כנסת ישראל היא בן זוגך", בראשית רבה פי"א

[126] שם משמואל חיי שרה תרע"ג "בו היינו שבת, ובשלוחו היינו בימי החול "

[127] רא"ש ב"ק ספ"ז "זמן עונה הוא בשבת, שנאמר ושמרו בני ישראל את השבת ר"ת ביאה."

[128] ס' יב

a mitzvah unto itself. It follows then that the blessing over it is a mitzvah blessing, as he writes[129]:

> כָּל הַמְקַדֵּשׁ אִשָּׁה בֵּין עַל יְדֵי עַצְמוֹ בֵּין עַל יְדֵי שָׁלִיחַ צָרִיךְ לְבָרֵךְ קֹדֶם הַקִּדּוּשִׁין אוֹ הוּא אוֹ שְׁלוּחוֹ כְּדֶרֶךְ שֶׁמְּבָרְכִין עַל כָּל הַמִּצְוֹת
> All who marry a woman, whether by oneself, or through a representative, need to bless before the kiddushin, either him or his representative, like the way that we bless on every mitzvah.

The gemara pivots slightly by shifting the source of מצוה בו יותר מבשלוחו to the later part of the mishnah dealing with women.

> איכא דאמרי בהא איסורא נמי אית בה כדרב יהודה אמר רב
> דאמר רב יהודה אמר רב אסור לאדם שיקדש את האשה עד שיראנה
> שמא יראה בה דבר מגונה ותתגנה עליו ורחמנא אמר (ויקרא יט, יח)
> ואהבת לרעך כמוך
> וכי איתמר דרב יוסף אסיפא איתמר האשה מתקדשת בה
> ובשלוחה השתא בשלוחה מיקדשא בה מיבעיא אמר רב יוסף מצוה בה
> יותר מבשלוחה כי הא דרב ספרא מחריך רישא רבא מלח שיבוטא
> אבל בהא איסורא לית בה כדל״ל דאמר ז״ל טב למיתב טן דו
> מלמיתב ארמלו

There are those who say that there is also a prohibition in this. As Rav Yehudah said in the name of Rav. For Rav Yehudah said in the name of Rav: It is forbidden for a man to betroth a woman until he sees her, lest he see something unseemly in her and she becomes repulsive to him. The Torah teaches: You shall love your fellow as yourself. When was Rav Yosef's teaching stated, it was stated in reference to the second part, "a woman can become betrothed

---

[129] פ״ג מאישות הכ״ג

> personally or through her agent." Now, if a woman can become betrothed through her agent, is it also necessary to teach that she can become betrothed by herself? Rav Yosef replied, It is a greater mitzvah personally than through her agent. As we find that Rav Safra singed the head, Rava would salt the fish. However, in this case there is no prohibition involved like Reish Lakish. Reish Lakish said "It is better to live as two together than to live alone."

It would then make sense that our gemara is referring to the hechsher mitzvah of oneg Shabbos. Consequently, this concept doesn't appear to be a part of the mitzvah itself, but rather an idea within broader spiritual practice[130].

If this is true, then a shofar or a lulav which are being kept in a distant place would see an individual shlepping there to be a fulfillment of this axiom, as opposed to sending someone else.

Alternatively, Rashi understands the actions of the Rabbis to be fulfilling an actual mitzvah, namely of honoring the shabbat.

מחריך רישא - לכבוד שבת:

How might we then understand the mitzvah in the mishnah? It would be inappropriate to support the concept of *מצוה בה יותר מבשלוחה*, in the context of a hechsher mitzvah, by showing the application of it the performance of an actual mitzvah. According to Maimonides, the Mishnah is referring to an actual mitzvah. He writes in the laws of marriage as follows[131]:

---

[130] ביד המלך (שבת פ"ל ה"ו) דלא מצינו הא מצוה בו יותר מבשלוחו רק בשני מצות, בקידושי אשה ובהכנת כבוד שבת. וכן בהגה חכמת שלמה (או"ח תס:ב)

[131] הלכות אישות ג:ט

> מִצְוָה שֶׁיְּקַדֵּשׁ אָדָם אֶת אִשְׁתּוֹ בְּעַצְמוֹ יוֹתֵר מֵעַל יְדֵי שְׁלוּחוֹ. וְכֵן מִצְוָה לָאִשָּׁה שֶׁתְּקַדֵּשׁ עַצְמָהּ בְּיָדָהּ יוֹתֵר מֵעַל יְדֵי שְׁלוּחָהּ.

He also understand the actions in the gemara to be a fulfillment of kavod Shabbos. In the laws of Shabbos he writes[132]:

> אַף עַל פִּי שֶׁהָיָה אָדָם חָשׁוּב בְּיוֹתֵר וְאֵין דַּרְכּוֹ לִקַּח דְּבָרִים מִן הַשּׁוּק וְלֹא לְהִתְעַסֵּק בִּמְלָאכוֹת שֶׁבַּבַּיִת חַיָּב לַעֲשׂוֹת דְּבָרִים שֶׁהֵן לְצֹרֶךְ הַשַּׁבָּת בְּגוּפוֹ שֶׁזֶּה הוּא כְּבוֹדוֹ.

Even though a person is exceedingly important, and it isn't their way to (personally) purchase things from the market, nor to be (personally) involved in the domestic duties of the house, still a person is obligated to do things which are for the needs of Shabbos, with oneself, for that is it's honor[133].

The Baal HaTanya observes an interesting word change in the Rambam from marriage to Shabbos and uses it to answer a question from the laws of honoring one's parents. The code of Jewish law teaches[134]:

> אָמַר לוֹ אָבִיו: הַשְׁקֵנִי מַיִם, וְיֵשׁ לְפָנָיו לַעֲשׂוֹת מִצְוָה עוֹבֶרֶת, כְּגוֹן קְבוּרַת מֵת אוֹ לְוָיָה, אִם אֶפְשָׁר לַמִּצְוָה שֶׁתֵּעָשֶׂה עַל יְדֵי אֲחֵרִים, יַעֲסֹק בִּכְבוֹד אָבִיו. וְאִם הִתְחִיל בַּמִּצְוָה תְּחִלָּה, יִגְמֹר, דְּהָעוֹסֵק בְּמִצְוָה פָּטוּר מִן הַמִּצְוָה (בֵּית יוֹסֵף בְּשֵׁם הר"ן). וְאִם אֵין שָׁם אֲחֵרִים לַעֲשׂוֹת, יַעֲסֹק בַּמִּצְוָה וְיַנִּיחַ כְּבוֹד אָבִיו. מִיהוּ אִם אֵין זְמַן הַמִּצְוָה עוֹבֶרֶת, יַעֲסֹק בִּכְבוֹד אָבִיו וְאַחַר כָּךְ יַעֲשֶׂה הַמִּצְוָה

---

[132] ל:ו

[133] It isn't clear if he is referring to Shabbos or the person.

[134] י"ד רמ:ב

If one's father asks one to draw water for them and there is an opportunity to do a mitzvah that won't be available later, for example a body that needs to be buried or a funeral, if it is possible to have someone else perform it, then involve yourself in fulfilling the honor of one's father. If a person had already started a mitzvah, finish it first, for one who is engaged in one mitzvah is exempt from another. And if there is no one else who can do the other mitzvah, then you should fulfill it and leave the honor of one's parent for the moment. However, if the other mitzvah will still be available later, then first honor one's parent.

So how was it halachically permissible for these great Rabbis to interrupt their learning to do something for Shabbos that others could have taken care of? He explains that it must be an obligation on the body (like tefillin), that no one else could do on our behalf.

Indeed the Rambam in the laws of Shabbos doesn't use the language of "mitzvah" like he does by marriage, but rather a language of "obligation"[135].

אַף עַל פִּי שֶׁהָיָה אָדָם חָשׁוּב בְּיוֹתֵר וְאֵין דַּרְכּוֹ לִקַּח דְּבָרִים מִן הַשּׁוּק וְלֹא לְהִתְעַסֵּק בִּמְלָאכוֹת שֶׁבַּבַּיִת חַיָּב לַעֲשׂוֹת דְּבָרִים שֶׁהֵן לְצֹרֶךְ הַשַּׁבָּת בְּגוּפוֹ שֶׁזֶּה הוּא כְּבוֹדוֹ.

Even if someone is an important person, who doesn't normally go out to buy things from the market, or engage in work in the home, a person is still obligated to do things which are for the needs of Shabbos, with their own body, for that is it's honor.

This presents two very significant problems in our

---

[135] ל:ו

sugya. Firstly, how can the gemara prove a concept of מצוה בו יותר מבשלוחו in regards to marriage in the mishnah, which is 'only' a "mitzvah," from rabbis that did things themselves for Shabbos out of an "obligation"? Maybe only in a situation of higher necessity do we apply this principle. Secondly, and much more fundamentally bothersome, is how can the Talmud try to teach the concept of "מצוה בו יותר מבשלוחו" from a situation that demands that the person themselves does the mitzvah and doesn't even allow for the possibility of using a messenger for it?! It is like trying to prove the principle by observing how we see that people put on tefillin themselves as opposed to having someone else represent them in the putting on of tefillin. The phrase "מצוה בו יותר מבשלוחו" implies that there is another option, it is just inferior. Here, according to the Rambam, there is no option to use a *shaliach*!

Rav Nosson Gestetner[136] offers a very satisfying and insightful approach. In the laws of ritual slaughter, the Rambam reminds us to perform mitzvot in a respectable way, because our attitude towards fulfilling the mitzvah is a reflection of how we relate to the one who commanded us to do it[137].

וּכְשֶׁמְּכַסֶּה לֹא יְכַסֶּה בְּרַגְלוֹ אֶלָּא בְּיָדוֹ אוֹ בְּסַכִּין אוֹ בִּכְלִי כְּדֵי שֶׁלֹּא יִנְהַג בּוֹ מִנְהַג בִּזָּיוֹן וְיִהְיוּ מִצְוֹת בְּזוּיוֹת עָלָיו. שֶׁאֵין הַכָּבוֹד לְעַצְמָן שֶׁל מִצְוֹת אֶלָּא לְמִי שֶׁצִּוָּה בָּהֶן בָּרוּךְ הוּא וְהִצִּילָנוּ מִלְּמַשֵּׁשׁ בַּחֹשֶׁךְ וְעָרַךְ אוֹתָנוּ נֵר לְיַשֵּׁר הַמַּעֲקַשִּׁים וְאוֹר לְהוֹרוֹת נְתִיבוֹת הַיֹּשֶׁר. וְכֵן הוּא אוֹמֵר (תהילים קיט: קה)
: נֵר לְרַגְלִי דְבָרֶךָ וְאוֹר לִנְתִיבָתִי

When one covers the blood, don't use one's foot

---

[136] להורות נתן מועדים ח'ה ד'כד

[137] ה' שחיטה יד:טז

but rather one's hand or a utensil in order not to be accustomed to dishonor the fulfillment of the mitzvah. For the honor isn't for the mitzvah itself, but rather for the one who has commanded us, may God be blessed, and has saved us from roaming in the darkness and prepared for us a candle and light to give us direction. (Psalm 119:105) Your word is a lamp for my feet and a light for my path.

The Magid Mishnah explains a little more about our connection to God though how we approach a mitzvah.

שלא יכסנו ברגל שלא יהיו המצות בזויות עליו כי כבוד המצות
כבוד הש"י שהם שלוחיו של מקום וכבוד הנשלח הוא כבוד השולח:

One shouldn't use their foot...because the honor of a mitzvah is the honor of God, in that they are emissaries of God and the honor of the one sent is the honor of the one sending them.

It seems clear that the Rambam understands that in every mitzvah there is an aspect of honor, as opposed to a global principle that might extend to good deeds in general. By choosing a mitzvah whose entirety is one of honor and teaching us that no one else is capable of fulfilling it on behalf of another, the Talmud highlights that it is the honor piece itself that is lost when we rely on another.

What comes out from this new understanding of *shlichut* (agency) is that although it is possible with certain mitzvos to have a representative fulfill the technical obligation, it is deemed a dishonorable discharging of the obligation, on some level, when we don't take it as an opportunity to connect to God directly with our own actions and honor God by being present for it.

Rashi, as mentioned, explains that when we do a

mitzvah with our own body we receive more reward. The Tosafot Ri HaZakein writes something similar[138]:

כל מצוה שמוטלת עליו יעשה בגופו ולא על ידי שליח.
Every mitzvah that is placed on a person, they should do it with their body and not through a messenger.

It would seem that Rashi intends to extend the principle beyond obligations which are placed on a person to perhaps even optional mitzvos that aren't placed on the person to perform. It would follow then, that Rashi sees this concept as external to the mitzvah itself and more like the teaching of[139] *אגרא צערא לפום*. According to the exertion is the reward. By contrast, the Tosafot Ri HaZakein sees this as part of the original obligation itself.

Rabbanu Chananel provides clarifying language on the Gemara in Shabbos.

כולהו כדמפרש בגמרא בריש האיש מקדש. שקיום המצוה באדם עצמו טפי עדיף יתר מבשלוחו.

The actual fulfillment of the mitzvah itself is greater when it is done in an embodied way.

Although "*מצוה בו יותר מבשלוחו*" doesn't appear in the parallel section in the Jerusalem Talmud, the two main commentaries there still read it into the mishnah and ostensibly quote Rashi's understanding. The *קרבן העדה* understands the order, as opposed to the redundancy, to be the source of the teaching. He writes:

---

[138] "Placed on" might imply commandments that we are obligated in, as opposed to ones we choose to fulfill.

[139] בספ"ה דאבות

> *בו תחלה, ואח"כ בשלוחו, וקמ"ל שמצוה בו יותר מבשלוחו,*
> *דכי עסיק הוא בעצמו במצוה מקבל שכר טפי*

In the *פני משה* we find a similar understanding, but expressed with new language. He writes:

> *לכתחילה בו, ואם לאו, בשלוחו שמצוה בו יותר מבשלוחו דכי*
> *עסיק גופיה במצוה מקבל שכר טפי*

Speaking about "*מצוה בו יותר מבשלוחו*" as an ideal makes it sound like a preference and certainly not an obligation. When the Jerusalem Talmud says "*ששלוחו של אדם כמותו*", it is fair to understand that the prefix "*כ,*" meaning "like," equates things as being so similar that they are considered as equals, but they are only "like" each other, not the thing itself.

There are a couple of difficulties in understanding Rashi's explanation of the concept of *מצוה בו יותר מבשלוחו* as being motivated by ways to gain more reward. Firstly, getting more reward is a consequence (*תוצאה*) of "*מצוה בו יותר מבשלוחו*", not the reason (*סיבה*) for the principal[140]. Secondly, we are taught in the famous teaching in Ethics of Our Fathers[141]:

> אַנְטִיגְנוֹס אִישׁ סוֹכוֹ קִבֵּל
> מִשִּׁמְעוֹן הַצַּדִּיק. הוּא הָיָה אוֹמֵר, אַל תִּהְיוּ כַעֲבָדִים הַמְשַׁמְּשִׁין אֶת
> הָרַב עַל מְנָת לְקַבֵּל פְּרָס, אֶלָּא הֱווּ כַּעֲבָדִים הַמְשַׁמְּשִׁין אֶת הָרַב שֶׁלֹּא עַל
> מְנָת לְקַבֵּל פְּרָס, וִיהִי מוֹרָא שָׁמַיִם עֲלֵיכֶם.

Antigonus, leader of Socho, received the tradition from Shimon the Righteous. He used to say: Be not like servants who serve their master for the

---

[140] עיין בדבר משה

[141] א:ג

sake of receiving a reward; instead be like servants who serve their master not for the sake of receiving a reward. And let the awe of Heaven be upon you.

Rav Gedalia Finkel asks a similar question from a seemingly contradictory Mishnah in Avos[142]. In the second chapter it teaches:

וֶהֱוֵי זָהִיר בְּמִצְוָה קַלָּה כְּבַחֲמוּרָה, שֶׁאֵין אַתָּה יוֹדֵעַ מַתַּן שְׂכָרָן שֶׁל מִצְוֹת.

Be as punctilious with a light mitzvah like you would with a strict mitzvah because we do not know the [true] reward for a mitzvah.

Which implies that if we did know the true reward for a mitzvah, then we would prioritize the ones that gave the most reward! He explains that the reward is just an indicator of the value, as God sees it, not a motivator for us to do the Divine will. This is also how he understands our Rashi-

וכעי"ז יש לפרש דברי רש"י בריש פ"ב דקידושין ד"ה מצוה בו יותר מבשלוחו - דבהא דמקבל שכר טפי הוא ראיה דחשיבא מצוה טפי.

According to this approach, Rashi also understands this to be limited to the fulfillment of a mitzvah, even if the mitzvah isn't placed on us, but one that we choose to perform, because when we do the mitzvah ourselves we do the mitzvah better, it is less of a fulfillment of the mitzvah to do it through a messenger. There is now no disagreement between the Rishonim as to whether this is part of a mitzvah, or an independent concept that would extend beyond mitzvos, except for the Ran.

---

[142] אמרי גדליה יבמות פתח דבר

By understanding our mishnah as referring to an act that enables the fulfillment of a mitzvah, it would appear that he holds this not to be limited to the mitzvah itself. Perhaps there is an alternative way to understand his intention. Rav Eliyahu Boruch Finkel argues that there is a distinction between marriage and other mitzvos in that there is no way to fulfill having children, in a halachically permissible way, outside of marriage and therefore it is an absolutely necessary step. By other mitzvahs, it is only circumstantial and not intrinsic that they happen to be far from a person. A person could come and blow the shofar or give a lulav and it wouldn't be necessary to go anywhere to fulfill the mitzvos.

The *נציב* makes a distinction between a hechsher mitzvah that the Torah mentions explicitly as it applies to "*מצוה בו יותר מבשלוחו*" [143]. He writes:

הרי העלינו דיש נפקא מינה בין מצות הכנה שכתובה בתורה דיש לה מעלה וזכות דמצוה בו יותר מבשלוחו לאפוקי הכנה שאינה כתובה בתורה

Since we learn marriage from a verse, even if it is only a hechsher mitzvah according to the Ran, it may still be elevated to a status higher than those not mentioned. Perhaps only with these specific ones is there an application of "*מצוה בו יותר מבשלוחו*" and, like the other Rishonim, this is not an external value.

Seeing *shlichut* (agency) through this lens removes the conflict of "*ברוב עם הדרת מלך*", because the goal is always to bring the most glory to God. The question is only in the discerning of when more glory is brought through one over the other. For example, if we understand the concept

---

[143] העמק שאלה ס' קס"ט

of "*ברוב עם הדרת מלך*", in a modern application of a presidential inauguration, the greater the crowd, the greater the glory. The opposite would also be true.

It is much less significant who the people are that show up as it is how many there are that do. So too by havdalah. Although each person's havdalah is unique and special, it isn't person specific. In such situations, there is more glory for God when there is unity and focus of the masses. However, when the contribution is person specific, like marriage, the honor is in showing up as one's self in relationship with another as in our relationship with God[144]. This perspective is additionally helpful in the prioritizing of who should represent others when it is appropriate to have a *shaliach*[145].

The Jerusalem Talmud doesn't contain the *sugya* of "*ברוב עם הדרת מלך*", even though the verse is quoted at least eight times in the Bavli. Perhaps the Jerusalem Talmud is less concerned about giving expression to the Divine Glory than the Babylonian simply because the Divine Presence is in exile, outside of Israel, and requires us to reveal it[146].

תניא ר"ש בן יוחי אומר בוא וראה כמה חביבין ישראל לפני הקב"ה

---

[144] עיין בשו"ת הרדב"ז (חלק ג' ס' תתקע"ז [תקמ"ו])

It is widely understood that chametz on Pesach is a metaphor for the evil inclination and therefore the searching for it, with the light of the Torah, is a very individual experience and obligation.

[145] עיין בתבואות שור סי' כ"ח סק"ד

who discusses giving a mitzvah to someone more important as a glorification of the mitzvah and not something dishonorable.

[146] מגילה כט.

שבכל מקום שגלו שכינה עמהן גלו למצרים שכינה עמהן שנאמר
(שמואל א ב, כז) הנגלה נגליתי לבית אביך בהיותם במצרים וגו' גלו
לבבל שכינה עמהן שנאמר (ישעיהו מג, יד) למענכם שלחתי בבלה ואף
כשהן עתידין ליגאל שכינה עמהן שנאמר (דברים ל, ג) ושב ה' אלהיך
את שבותך והשיב לא נאמר אלא ושב מלמד שהקב״ה שב עמהן מבין
הגליות

It was taught in a Baraita: Rabbi Shimon Ben Yochai says: 'Come and see how beloved Israel are before God, be blessed! Wherever they were exiled, the Divine Presence is with them. As it is said: Wasn't I revealed to your father's house when they were in Egypt...They were exiled to Babylon and the Divine Presence was with them as it is said: For your sake I was sent to Babylon...And also when they are destined to be redeemed, the Divine Presence will be with them, as it is said: And Hashem will return with your returning exiles. It doesn't say 'that God will bring back' but rather that 'God will return'. It teaches that the Holy One, blessed be God, will return with them from the exile.

The Gemara continues to explore the more exact location of the Shechinah in Bavel.

(יחזקאל יא, טז) ואהי להם למקדש מעט אמר רבי יצחק אלו בתי
כנסיות ובתי מדרשות שבבבל ולא אמר זה בית רבינו שבבבל דרש רבא
מאי דכתיב (תהלים צ, א) ה' מעון אתה היית לנו אלו בתי כנסיות ובתי
מדרשות אמר אביי מריש הואי גריסנא בביתא ומצלינא בבי כנשתא כיון
דשמעית להא דקאמר דוד (תהלים כו, ח) ה' אהבתי מעון ביתך הואי
גריסנא בבי כנישתא.

Yet I have been for them a minor sanctuary. Reb Yitzchak said: These are the synagogues and study halls in Babylon; and R' Elazar said: This refers to the house of our teacher in Babylon. Rava explained: What is meant by 'Hashem! You have been an abode for us?' These are the synagogues and study halls. Abaye said: Originally I would study at home and pray in the synagogues. Once I understood what King David wrote: Hashem! I love the abode of your house, I started to study in synagogues.

Seeing how the Babylonian Talmud sees the study of Torah as a revelation of the Divine Presence, and consequently the Divine Glory, perhaps this can help with some of the textual variations in the Tosefta. Tosefta K'Pshuta writes[147]

גורס בדברי ב"ש וב"ה כבתוספתא שלפנינו, ומסיים ודוקא בבית המדרש, דאיכא בטל תורה אבל במסיב, אחד מברך לכולם. ובפיסקי ר ישעיה האחרון אחד מברך לכולן שנ' ברוב עם הדרת מלך ... ואם הן יושבין בבית המדרש, כל אחד מברך לעצמו מפני ביטול ביהמ"ד.

The language of "Nullifying the Beit Medrash" is now not about solo Jewish practice or the inconvenience that interrupting learning provides, but is very specifically about engaging with the Divine presence predicated on the awareness that God is in the study hall. In the Tosefta, which omits the word "*יושבין*" "sitting," Beit Shammai sees just being there, passively, as being enhanced by doing a mitzvah together, whereas Beit Hillel encourages individuals to be proactive and own the mitzvah themselves. Perhaps these positions reverse when, in the Bavli, it is explicitly about the nullification of learning. When people are already showing up in service, through learning, Beit Shammai doesn't want to break the focus of the individual who is already connected in the awareness of the Divine Presence through learning, whereas Beit Hillel want people to upgrade their focus from an individual revelation to a communal one.

In relationships, it's essential to understand what is

---

[147] תשה"ג גיאוניקא (הוצ' הר"ל גינצבורג עמ, 262; אוה"ג התשובות עמ' 127)

important to the other and to take those things seriously. The Torah contains the details of what is important to God and how we are meant to prioritize competing interests. The more that we study Torah, the better we are able to understand God and how to be a better partner in our relationship with God, each other, and the world.

When we see social justice as our spiritual practice, it is helpful to explore how the rabbis of the Talmud prioritized and balanced the solo and communal contributions in religious life. The more that we can find and create opportunities where it wouldn't be the same without us, the greater the contribution of our individualized self, even in community.

CREDITS

Congregation Beit Simchat Torah and Rabbi Mike Moskowitz are grateful to all those who have granted permission to reprint previously published material in *Textual Activism* (2019).

"Answering the Transgender Son": Reprinted by permission of the New York Jewish Week Jewish Orthodox Feminist Alliance blog, where the article originally appeared attributed to the pen name Kol Raychaim.

"Not Everything is As It Appears": Reprinted by permission of co-author Seth M. Marnin and the Times of Israel Blogs, where the article originally appeared.

"Redeeming Religion from Slavery": Reprinted by permission of Tikkun, where the article originally appeared.

"A Passover Message from the Southern Border": Reprinted by permission of co-author Rabbi Yael Rapport, who originally delivered it as a drashah at Congregation Beit Simchat Torah.

"All Who Were Silenced, Let Them Come Speak": Reprinted by permission of co-author Shari Motro, riginally published as "How To Host a Truly Inclusive Passover Seder."

"Hillula to Her Heart": Reprinted by permission of Tikkun, where the article originally appeared.

"Transgender and Transcendent": Reprinted by permission of the New York Jewish Week Jewish Orthodox Feminist Alliance blog, where the article originally appeared attributed to the pen name Kol Raychaim.

"Cisgender Humility and Accepting the Torah": Reprinted by permission of the New York Jewish Week Jewish Orthodox Feminist Alliance blog, where the article originally appeared.

"Rabbinic Responsibility for LGBTQ Jews": Reprinted by permission of the Congregation Beit Simchat Torah website (cbst.org), where the article originally appeared.

"Rosh Chodesh and Rabbisplaining": Reprinted by permission of the New York Jewish Week Jewish Orthodox Feminist Alliance blog, where the article originally appeared.

"9th of Av Letter to Day Schools": Reprinted by permission of co-author Deborah Megdal.

"Rosh Hashanah: A Time for Divine Consent": Reprinted by permission of the New York Jewish Week Jewish Orthodox Feminist Alliance blog, where the article originally appeared.

"Coming of Age as Gender Non-Conforming": Reprinted by permission of co-author Rabbi Yael Rapport and the New York Jewish Week Jewish Orthodox Feminist Alliance blog, where the article originally appeared.

"Expanding the 'We' For Rosh Hashanah": Reprinted by permission of co-author Rebecca Krevat and the Hitoreri blog, where the article originally appeared.

"Sukkot, Security, and Transgender Rights": Reprinted by permission of co-author Seth M. Marnin and the Keshet blog on My Jewish Learning, where the article originally appeared.

"The Cloud of Glory": Reprinted by permission of the Keshet blog on My Jewish Learning, where the article originally appeared attributed to the pen name Kol Raychaim.

"Building a Temple from Tears": Reprinted by permission of the Bayit Builder's Blog, where the article originally appeared.

"Coming Together Against Hate": Reprinted by permission of co-author Rabbi Sharon Kleinbaum and OUT, where the article originally appeared with the title "Antisemitism and LGBTQ+ Hate are Spiking – So We Must Come Together."

"Renewal & Rebirth": Reprinted by permission of the Keshet blog on My Jewish Learning, where the article originally appeared with the title "Reflections from an Orthodox Rabbi Shunned for Being LGBTQ-Friendly."

"Back to the Garden: Purim, Patriarchy, and a Path Forward": - Reprinted by permission of co-author Rabba Wendy Amsellem and the New York Jewish Week Jewish Orthodox Feminist Alliance blog, where the article originally appeared.

"I Am a Boy and These Are My Clothes": Reprinted by permission of the New York Jewish Week Jewish Orthodox Feminist Alliance blog, where the article originally appeared.

"Noah's Ark: A Failed Ally-ship": - Reprinted by permission of the Bayit Builder's Blog, where the article originally appeared.

"Allyship as Spiritual Practice": Reprinted by permission of the Velveteen Rabbi Blog, where the article originally appeared,

"Advancing the Rabbinic Prescription For Transgender Health Care": Reprinted by permission of co-atuhor Dr. Joshua Safer and Fresh Ideas from Hadassah-Brandeis Institute (HBI), where the article originally appeared.

"Shabbos Shows Us How to 'Chaver Up'": Reprinted by permission of co-author Seth M. Marnin and the Times of Israel Blogs, where the article originally appeared.

"What the Torah and Talmud Teach Us About Calling Transgender People By Their Names": Reprinted by permission of co-author Seth Marnin and Tablet, where the article originally appeared.

"Queer Advice from Straight Rabbis": Reprinted by permission of co-author Rabbi Yael Rapport, originally appeared with the title "7 Ways Straight Jews Can Become Better LGBTQ Allies."

"I'm an Orthodox Rabbi Marching with Pride": Reprinted by permission of the New York Jewish Week Jewish Orthodox Feminist Alliance blog, where the article originally appeared.

"One Straight, White, Cisgender Rabbi's Role as an Ally": Reprinted by permission of Auburn Theological Seminary, on whose site the article originally appeared.

"Wrestling with Mourning on Transgender Day of

Remembrance": Reprinted by permission of co-author Seth M. Marnin and The Times of Israel Blogs, where the article originally appeared.

"World AIDS Day and the Role of the Righteous": Reprinted by permission of co-author Jesse Katz.

"In Dark Times, Be a Light": Reprinted by permission of co-authors Rabbi Rachel Barenblat and Victoria Cook, and eJewish Philanthropy, where the article originally appeared.

"How Goodly are Your Rainbow Tents": Reprinted by permission of co-author Lizzie Stein and ReformJudaism.org, where the article originally appeared.

"The Torah of Action": Reprinted by permission of the Keshet blog on My Jewish Learning, where the article originally appeared.

"It's a Big Torah": Reprinted by permission of the Keshet blog on My Jewish Learning, where the article originally appeared attributed to the pen name Kol Raychaim and with the title "Reflections from an Orthodox Rabbi with a Trans Child."

"Corruption and Greed Get in the Way of the Torah": Reprinted by permission of The Forward, where the article originally appeared with the title "In Lakewood, Sometimes Corruption And Greed Get In The Way Of The Torah."

"Orthodox Jews and the Child Victims Act": Reprinted by permission of The Forward, where the article originally appeared with the title "Why On Earth Are Orthodox Jews Opposing The Child Victims Act?"

"Healing the Afflictions of Separation": Reprinted by

permission of the Bayit Builder's Blog, where the article originally appeared.

"Interfaith Leaders Stand Up for Yes on 3 Campaign": Reprinted with the permission of co-author Reverend Stephanie Kendell and Medium, where the article originally appeared.

"The Audacious and Inspirational Gift of Pride": Reprinted by the permission of co-author Reverend Amy Butler and Tikkun, where the article originally appeared.

"Opening Doors and Hearts on Transgender Day of Visibility": Reprinted with the permission of co-author Reverend Amy Butler and Baptist News, where the article originally appeared with the title "Transgender Day: A Chance for Churches to Open Doors and Hearts To Our Transgender Neighbors."

"Faith Leaders Must Stop Acting As If There's No Preventing Natural Disasters": Reprinted by the permission of co-author Reverend Amy Butler and Religion News Service, where the article originally appeared.

"Religiously Non-Conforming – Unorthodox Podcast": Reprinted by the permission of Tablet's Unorthodox Podcast, which originally aired the interview in the episode "Kung Fu Naches."

"The Rabbinic Voice of Allyship – Here and Now": Reprinted by permission of WBUR and NPR's "Here and Now," which originally aired the interview with the title "This Ultra-Orthodox Rabbi Says His Holiest Moment Was Becoming Public LGBTQ Ally."

Made in the USA
Monee, IL
13 September 2019